AF305244

NIKITA GALE

END OF SUBJECT

CLARION

NIKITA GALE

Curator's Note: Adult Contemporary
Ebony L. Haynes

In September 2021, Anita Baker confirmed via Twitter that she had regained control of her master recordings, posting, "All my children are coming home." Many Baker fans and fellow artists had been vocal about her having taken a stand against music streaming services, so this notable moment felt like a triumph. The following winter, Nikita Gale's *END OF SUBJECT* opened as the second exhibition at 52 Walker. Gale's work is the performance, similar to how Baker's work comprises lyrics and instrumentation. The performance of *END OF SUBJECT*, however, depends upon physical objects in space as they interact with sound, light, and an audience, and, as a result, documenting this type of work becomes more complex than the creation of master recordings.

END OF SUBJECT proposes a world where the very systems and structures we rely on to situate ourselves are disrupted or collapsed, and then it asks: What new arrangements and systems can we build out of these ruins? Here, the ruins of the performance are witnessed and represented both inside and outside the space—the viewer represents and embodies the experience, and any expectations are mediated and shaped through existing social and political systems. These systems and institutions, which we rely on to anchor our place in the world, often present an illusion of stability.

Together, the works in the show consider the phenomenological limits of performance: If you don't watch a performance, does it *perform*? There is a degree of separation when we try to document performance. The documentation is a secondary experience: the plates in this book cannot equate to what a physical body realizes in the space. Different angles, shifting light, and multi-channel sound may be documented; color washing over your body, or the way you discern timing and cadence, are less easily archived.

As an installation, *END OF SUBJECT* disrupts the assumption of how a space should be experienced, what goes in a gallery, and how people should behave as they enter an exhibition. The performance is nonnarrative, but there are clear starts and ends to its different parts. Many visitors wanted access to the timing, in order to make sure they saw the full two and a half hours, which includes twelve vignettes and twelve intermissions, all differing in length and offering disparate connections. Adding to their frustration, where the performance begins each day does not necessarily indicate the beginning of the work.

When a small, invited group arrived in the gallery after-hours for a group-relations exercise led by Andrea Fraser, new possibilities for documenting the performance came into play. The gathering involved recording and synthesizing how bodies move in the space and embody the performance, how observing participants' body language or hearing their meditations might influence one's own experience. Fraser's text presents a possible method of documenting the experience of the performance and reflects not on how an audience should behave but rather how an audience feels compelled to behave.

In line with explorations of performance documentation, Harmony Holiday offers her reflections on an iconic performer. (Here it is not Anita Baker but Tina Turner who analogizes the possible documentation and embodiment of performance.) Holiday's verses in "Suite for Tina Turner" are the poetic ruins of an experience. The poems capture one body's archive of witnessing sound, feeling a dance, hearing the motion onstage or on-screen. The spacing of the text evokes a suggested cadence of sound, perhaps the same that Holiday feels from Turner. Notes such as "(music here)" create an almost transcribed experience in listening—depending on who is doing the listening or audiencing, of course.

Between the materials and elements of a performance there is a tacit agreement that both enables the act of experiencing and relies on the act of viewing. Does the subject have to be in the space for the performance to happen? Does the video play when no one watches? Since the site of performance exists, there must be subjects to activate it—even though it is the end of the subject.

Are?! You?! Ready?!
Nikita Gale's *END OF SUBJECT*
Andrea Fraser

"What lies between the bodies and the sounds and the stage and the lights—what are we to each other in the act of witnessing? What have we agreed upon through the mere act of showing up?"[1]
—Nikita Gale

It's a cold Sunday afternoon in February 2022. I arrive at 52 Walker to facilitate a convening in Nikita Gale's exhibition *END OF SUBJECT*. The gallery, usually closed to the public on Sundays, has been opened for our gathering. The exhibition has been turned on and is running through its two-and-a-half-hour program of light and sound. As we greet one another individually, in pairs, and in small groups, music starts to play over the speakers.

Audio: polyphonic synthesizer music that sounds like an organ, with coughing at random moments.

We are mostly old friends with relationships linked through the artist. While only a few of us are strangers to one another, the masks we wear make it challenging to recognize each other. COVID-19 vaccine cards are checked by gallery staff. As we mill around, the amplified sound of someone walking around a room comes over the speakers, followed by a voice reading a list of symptoms. I hear the voice as the voice of a white male from the southern United States.

Fever; chills; cough; shortness of breath or difficulty breathing; fatigue; muscle or body aches; headache; new loss of taste or smell; sore throat; congestion or runny nose; nausea or vomiting; diarrhea; trouble breathing; persistent pain or pressure in the chest; new confusion; inability to wake or stay awake; pale gray- or blue-colored skin, lips, or nail beds, depending on skin tone.

Audio: baby laughing, dog barking, loud electronic glitch, a person running and breathing heavily; synth organ music reenters and fades out.

Some members of the group hurry downstairs to use the bathroom. Others walk around the gallery, taking in the show. A rumbling bass sound plays. A few more people arrive. The gallery staff ask whether the front door should be locked to avoid interruptions. The artist and I decide to leave it unlocked.

Audio: synth organ music.

Spotlights illuminate and scan the room to highlight different objects in the gallery space. They focus on six sets of metal bleachers, some partially crushed, others turned on their sides. As the organ music fades out, six different voices begin repeating a series of phrases.

Make some noise!

I can't heaaaar you!

Let me hear you make some noise!

Are?! You?! Ready?!

Put your hands together!

Touch down!

GOAL! GOOOAAAAALLLLLL!

Ladies annnnnd gentlemen!

Ladies annnnnd gentlemen!

Ladies annnnnnnnnnd gentlemen!

Stand clear of the closing doors.

Please turn off all electronic devices.

The captain has turned on the seatbelt sign.

Please make sure that all seats are in the upright position.

Audio: frightened whimpering, then a cat purring, fades into a loud engine noise and frightened, frantic breathing; synth organ music reenters and fades out.

At 4:30 p.m. the artist gathers the group near the front desk, introduces me, and explains that

I have been invited to contribute an essay to the catalogue for the show. I proposed this event to generate material for my text.[2] The artist informs the group that by participating in the event, they are consenting to being named as participants and to being anonymously paraphrased in my text.[3]

I step forward to the artist's side and begin to address the group.

Thank you, Nikita, for that introduction and for inviting me to do this. And thank you all for coming this afternoon to engage with Nikita's show, *END OF SUBJECT*, as a group.

The primary task of this group is to learn about what the exhibition is, means, and, above all, what it *does*. I understand what art *does* primarily in terms of what and how art activates structures and relationships in its context and as we encounter it. Those structures and relationships include—

I am interrupted by a voice over the speakers. I hear the voice as a white male voice with a British accent. The sound of a heartbeat can be heard in the background.

Stand with your feet together. Keep your arms relaxed at your sides.

Step out with your right foot. Your feet should now be about shoulders' width apart.

Step your left foot behind and to the right of your right foot. Your legs should now be crossing one another.

Step out with your right foot. Your feet should once again be shoulders' width apart.

Place your left foot back in its original position so that you are now standing with your feet together. The speed of the steps will be based on the rhythm of the song you are dancing to.

Repeat the steps, this time moving to the left.

Stand with your feet together. Keep your arms relaxed at your sides. Step forward about one and a half feet with your right foot.

Slide, or shuffle, your left foot up to meet your right foot. At least part of your foot should be touching the ground the entire time.

Step forward once again with your right foot. This is the last step of the sequence.

Repeat the move starting with your left foot. Step forward with your left foot about one and a half feet. Slide your right foot up to meet your left foot. Step forward again with your left foot.

Practice doing this move to the front, to the back (stepping backward), and side to side.

Stand with your feet together. Kick your right foot forward a few inches above the ground, then lean forward and step on the ball of that foot, but only for a second.

Place your foot back in its original position. Then step down with your left foot.

Repeat the move beginning with your left foot.

Some members of the group attempt to follow the dance instructions, stepping forward and back. Others stand still, listening, looking at the exhibition and at one another. I feel frozen. I stand still, holding my notes. I am amused by the synchronicity of the interruption, but also anxious. I feel displaced. My role and authority to lead this group has been usurped. The heartbeat in the audio quickens. The dance instruction ends.

Audio: a microphone being dragged underwater.

I continue my introduction.

Those structures and relationships include the physical, perceptual, and formal; they include structures of meaning; they include social structures, economic structures, and psychological and emotional structures; and they include structures of identity, which

combine many of these other structures. They include any structures we might become aware of as we engage with the exhibition, and they include many structures that we may not be aware of—that remain unconscious or unthought—but which may, nevertheless, be active and *enacted* as we respond to the exhibition.

Your task, as a member of this group, is to experience the exhibition and to reflect on and articulate what the exhibition activates in you. My task is to reflect on and articulate how the group as a whole may be *enacting* what the exhibition is activating.

I will hold this space of experiencing and reflecting until 6:00 p.m. For this period of time, I will consider everything that happens in this room, and everything that emerges in this group, as being activated by the exhibition.

I conclude my introduction and look out at the group. No one moves. The group seems to be waiting for something else to happen or for further instructions, uncertain about their task. Was there something else I should have said to make this clearer? Tension builds. What will happen when we enter the installation itself? What will happen when we put our bodies in the work? Are we ready to be subject to it? Are we ready to take up the roles it creates for us?

Finally, the artist moves toward the exhibition space. Others follow at a slight distance, as if the artist's body marks a boundary that no one wants to cross. The group takes a configuration reminiscent of a search party line formed to comb a large area for a missing person.

Two group members stay behind, between the first set of bleachers and the metal column closest to the street. I have the impression that they are taking cover there from some sort of threat. This is dispelled by their laughter. The exhibition has split off this pair to hold something it is activating: a sense of lightness, conviviality, and play, which contrasts with the general sense of tension and anxiety.

The exhibition scatters the group around the room. Group members carefully navigate tangles of electrical cords hanging down from the ceiling and snaking around the floor. Some people are drawn to the aluminum panels on the walls, which have words scratched into them and are partially illuminated by spotlights fixed to their surfaces. Others are drawn to the bleachers distributed through the space in various states of disarrangement and destruction. The gallery appears to me like the scene of a forensic investigation undertaken after a disaster.

Slowly, people move toward the center of the room and the group forms a loose circle. The circle tightens as someone finally begins to speak. The group becomes still and silent to catch her words. But just as she starts to speak, audio begins to play over the speakers. It sounds to me like a dog running around, panting, and objects being unloaded. Then a voice begins reading a series of questions. I hear the voice as a black female voice. As she speaks, the other sounds can still be heard in the background. A white male voice says, "Put it here." The dog barks. The man says, "Good boy."

> Do you feel that you're an outside observer of your thoughts, feelings, your body or parts of your body—for example, as if you were floating in air above yourself?

> Do you feel like a robot or that you're not in control of your speech or movements?

> Do you sense that your body, your legs or arms, appear distorted, enlarged, or shrunken, or that your head is wrapped in cotton?

> Do you experience emotional or physical numbness of your senses or responses to the world around you?

> Do you sense that your memories lack emotion, and that they may or may not be your own memories?

> Do you experience feelings of being alienated from or unfamiliar with your surroundings—for example, like you're living in a movie or a dream?

> Do you experience a feeling of emotional disconnection from people you care about, as if you were separated by a glass wall?

> Do your surroundings appear distorted, blurry, colorless, two-dimensional, or artificial, or do you have a heightened awareness and clarity of your surroundings?

> Do you experience distortions in perception of time, such as recent events feeling like the distant past?

> Do you experience distortions of distance and the size and shape of objects?

The voice stops speaking. The sound of a stream of liquid comes over the speakers. Is it someone peeing?

The group member resumes her comment, now with a touch of irony. She reports that she feels quite calm, rather than nervous—which is how she expected she would feel.

The exhibition seems to have given the group permission to relieve itself of what has been building up within it. Other members follow up by offering readings of different aspects of the show. One suggests that the audio we just heard is a description of dissociation. Another reflects on the arrangement of the bleachers, evoking choreography. A third member describes the bleachers as barricades, recalling a sense that one of them served as a privacy screen for the pair chatting separately while others moved into the space.

While the shared task of engaging with the exhibition constitutes the assembled individuals as a group, the exhibition itself seems to exert a counterforce, fragmenting and dispersing the group and dissociating group members from one another and perhaps even from themselves. Investigating, reading, and interpreting the exhibition become means to hold the group and self together against these forces of fragmentation. Yet the exhibition also activates a joining that not only escapes this fragmentation but is facilitated and protected by it. This joining is enacted by the chatting pair, who also seem to be holding the group's fantasy of what the exhibition wants, and from whom.

A group member calls attention to the aluminum panels on the walls, naming them "body prints" and linking their location on the periphery of the space and the words scratched into them—including the names of body parts—to a sense of dismemberment. One of the members, who had held back to chat with another member, disagrees and shares a sense of feeling grounded by the panels on the walls.

The group has taken up the task of describing itself as it has been constituted by the exhibition. It is a body in fragments, its members dismembered and dispersed, flung to the outer walls by a force that leaves only prints as traces of their impact, clues to be deciphered by others. And yet these panels also take possession of the boundary, which holds and contains the group, protecting it from dangerous shocks, like an electrical ground.

The apparently contradictory experiences of anxiety and calm, dismemberment and grounding, represent coordinates of the structures activated by the exhibition—coordinates that are indexed, like landmarks on a map, in the bodies of the different group members who feel them. On the most basic level, they index the experience, or potential experience, or memory, of pleasure and pain. These are the cardinal points of embodied experiencing: their foundational binary, which orients the emotional charge of all other binaries—from inside–outside to self–other, same–different, active–passive, subject–object, feminine–masculine, black–white—with the relational vector of sought and avoided and the moral, ethical, political, or aesthetic value of good and bad, right and wrong. These exist not as alternatives to each other but rather as coordinates of the structures active in the room,

activated by the exhibition, to be drawn with the bodies in which they register and colored with the thoughts and feelings they manifest.

Audio: synth organ music.

The music playing over the speakers disperses the group again. I think of the metaphor of the exhibition playing the group like an instrument, but it feels more like an organism than an organ—or like an organ in an anatomical sense, breathing the group in and out and circulating it around the room. When the music stops, the group slowly returns to its previous formation as a loose circle in the center of the room.

A group member describes feeling relief in how the sound provides direction. He refers to the dance instructions that interrupted the introduction at the start of the convening. Another group member connects the theme of instruction to an analysis of how the words on the aluminum panels interpolate the viewer, evoking the theory of how ideology functions through subjectivation and identity formation. A group member speaking for the first time shares the expectation that the audio will interrupt him as soon as he starts to speak and wonders how the group is constituting itself through speaking. Another member shares that he finds silence stressful and wonders whether the artist considers the white noise created by devices in the room as part of the work's score.

I am aware that four of the five members of the group who I perceive as male have just spoken, one after the other. They have been constituted as a subgroup and mobilized to speak as such by the structures activated by the exhibition. As this subgroup speaks to the dynamics of instruction and interruption, direction and subjection, they enact how these relations of, and to, authority and power intersect with gender, and specifically with masculinity. Authority is linked to identity, sound, voice, and speech. It provides relief, even a sense of safety. It interrupts and intrudes, but it also constitutes. Indeed, it has the group performing in a kind of magical synchronicity with the score. Finally, this authority is also linked to whiteness: Is the whiteness in the room to be associated with an anxious silence, or a silent power, or with the intervening presence of the artist and the work? Has it been conceptualized by the artist as a part of the work?

As I am considering how to speak to these dynamics, a group member I perceive as gender nonbinary speaks for the first time. They describe feeling unstable and the desire to sit down on the floor, linking this to childhood experiences in kindergarten. As they finish speaking, the lights dim. The group disperses.

Audio: distorted bass synthesizer.

A member of the group sits on one of the bleachers in the space. After the bass synthesizer sounds subside, another member of the group shares that she has spent a significant amount of time in the exhibition and how this gives her a different perspective from those who have not spent as much time in the show. Another group member describes being split between feelings of pleasure and pain. Silence ensues. Group members shift around the room, gradually and seemingly unconsciously closing in around the artist. The member who spoke to her extensive experience with the exhibition wonders if her comment has silenced the group.

Another form of authority has emerged in the group, an authority that intersects with the authority linked to gender and race but which also displaces it. It is authority rooted not in what we are but what we have in varying degrees: time, knowledge, and access to specific spaces and specific experiences, as insiders and outsiders. Who does the exhibition authorize to speak about it, to engage with it? Who does it let in? The group seems to be struggling with what parts of itself are welcome and safe to bring to the shared task of engaging with the exhibition, a task that demands differentiation as well as joining. When authority speaks, must it always also

silence and exclude? Must difference and joining always split into pleasure and pain?

The artist steps out of the center of the circle.

A group member reflects on how he is avoiding talking about the metal panels on the walls.

How is the exhibition structuring avoidance, and of what?

A member of the group associates the carving of the metal panels and the destruction of the bleachers with noisy high school sports and dances. Another group member associates this to talent shows and the tense feeling of anticipation while waiting for an event to start. Another reflects on wanting to lavish in the spectacle presented by the exhibition but also feeling dialed back. Yet another describes the exhibition as a fun space.

The exhibition has activated longings to revisit pleasurable experiences of joining in groups. However, rather than allowing for release, it is suspending the group in a space of tension between emotional regression and artistic sublimation. It activates an impulse to discharge tension in action, but also the countervailing impulse to exercise restraint, perhaps to avoid what regression may unleash: the violence of destruction and also exclusion. As I begin to articulate this reflection to the group, I am interrupted by the sounds of electronic blips and chirping birds, followed by what I hear as an electronically distorted female voice with a French accent. I raise my voice to be heard over the exhibition audio.

I'm the reason your mama tells you to come in at night
Yeah I'm the reason people got curfews
I'm the reason
Ha ha ha
I'm the reason you tuck your purse in tight, bitch
I'm the reason you lock your door
Yeah, yeah
I scare you

Fuck what you talking about 'cause you won't get
  on it
I'm the reason you call the police when you hear
  your next-door neighbor's dog barking
I'm the reason you lock your door
Fuck you
Yeah
Talk all that
I'm the reason
I scare you
I will leave my door open for you and you won't
  come in
Shut the fuck up
I'm that man
I'm that man, bitch, that you are scared of at night
Yeah so shut up
Don't talk all that shit now you're getting scared
I'm that man
Ha ha
Bitch, I'm the reason
I'm the reason, motherfuckers
Yeah
Just know that you lock your doors at night
  because of me
You goddamn right
I live off that

*Audio: electronic blips layered with rain, synth
organ music, a baby laughing.*

As I listen to the audio, I notice that the people
in the group whom I perceive as black have
moved to equal distances from one another,
forming a square within the circle of the group.
As the sound plays, the artist breaks this square
and moves away from the circle.

The group member who evoked high school
dances returns to a reflection on the installation as a theatrical staging. Another member
describes the installation as a mixture of
artifacts that evoke municipal gathering places.
A third member suggests that the bleachers
invite visitors to take the position of spectators,
turning the space into a stage and everyone
in it into performers. A fourth member links
these associations to art-historical debates that
dismissed minimalist art as theatrical and then
links these debates to homophobic violence and
to the power held by the gallery the exhibition

is in. Another member says she is avoiding
talking because she doesn't want to be cut off by
the audio. She links this to the anxiety of being
embarrassed and the desire to say smart things.

The audio seems to reverberate through the group
as a series of reversals and displacements. The
aspects of the exhibition described as theatrical
are functioning to contain the tensions that it
activates, priming the group to experience these
as a matter of staging and artifacts, as relations of
spectator and performer rather than interpersonal
and social antagonists, victims and perpetrators.
But this theatricality is not impermeable to the
here and now of the exhibition in its context
and the experiences of group members within it.
The sense of staging presents an allegory of that
here and now, which group members work with
to metabolize their experience, to make sense
of it, to symbolize it, and to think it—as well as
to escape thinking it. It does not block out the
sense of power activated by the exhibition, which
includes its context, and the violence of that
power as a power to define, include and exclude,
value and shame. Nor does it block out the sense
of vulnerability to that power.

A group member observes that the audio seems
to silence some voices in the group, while others
keep talking and speak louder to be heard. As
this member finishes speaking, the exhibition
audio starts to play again. An electronic thumping
sound is layered with a number of different voices
speaking over one another. A couple of group
members sit down on the floor as the audio plays.

  I
THERE I AM
Me
THERE I AM
Mine
THERE I AM
My
THERE I AM
You
THERE I AM
Your
THERE I AM

Yours
THERE I AM
Us
THERE I AM
Our
THERE I AM
We
THERE I AM
Ours
THERE I AM
Them
THERE I AM
They
THERE I AM
Their
THERE I AM
Theirs

Audio: synth organ music.

As the voices peter out and the thumping stops, a group member notes that the bleachers didn't make her think of high school. She reflects that she might have repressed this association because her high school was very elitist and competitive and always made her feel out of place. Another group member notes a split in different forms of viewing: the free, autonomous, individual viewer versus the collective viewer or the audience as a group. He also notes that the references to art history make him feel resentful. He contrasts the visible cabling that forms part of the sculptural elements of the installation and the intentionally hidden wiring, describing the resources required to hide cabling as "power in the walls." Another group member insists that the installation is FUN. He loves it. But nevertheless, he feels anxious. Another group member speaks of her frustration that the group isn't doing more with the exhibition. Another group member evokes the word "selfish," which appears on one of the metal panels. Another group member talks about how the lights create cinematic scenes in which the members become actors, making her feel like she is watching a movie. Another group member talks about the pleasure of feeling worked over by the show. Another group member reflects that she's having a hard time feeling settled and has been reluctant to put down her bag. She wants to

be near the bleachers that are the most smashed. Unlike the other bleachers, being near these feels like a full break.

Does the exhibition want the group to join together in competition? Or in love? Does it want the group to join together at all? Or does it want the group members to remain a collection of autonomous individuals, with different degrees of access to the power it holds and different degrees of place, who watch one another from a distance, as if in different worlds? The exhibition seems to be holding the group in between, in a longing to be in the break.

The lights come on and the room turns magenta.

Audio: whistling, a baby crying, people laughing, a baby laughing, musical tones, people crying, and a toilet flushing.

A few group members sit on the bleachers as the audio plays. Another group member kneels on the ground. The artist has moved out of the installation and away from the group.

A group member comments that it feels like the work is trolling the audience. Another group member describes a sense of being suspended between abjection and joy. The work feels too stylish to be totally abject. Another group member returns to earlier discussions of choreography. Another group member talks about sounds she associates with peeing, leaking, and water dripping, and notes that she has been squatting. She asks, "What do you want us to do?"

The lights go out.

Audio: distorted bass synthesizer.

A group member says that it's not so bad to be interrupted. Another group member points out that the people sitting on the bleachers are sitting on art. Another member says they feel very aware of the other bodies in the space. They

point to another group member and say they
have no idea who that person is. They speak to
an experience of differentiation and describe
the metal panels on the walls as body prints that
protest against being legible.

I wonder if the group is now performing the
end of subject. There is a sense of dissolution, of
the illegibility of bodies and their social identi-
ties, of the permeability of their boundaries.

A group member expresses a sense of confusion,
referring to the audio but rendering "there I am"
as "what I am." He describes reaching for something "pre-felt." Another member associates this
with the heartbeat that played in the background
of the choreography instructions at the start of
the convening. Another member takes up the
theme of social identity and describes being
very aware that the artist is a black artist. As a
man in the group, he is very aware of how much
he speaks. As a black man, he has a sense of
responsibility to respond to the work as a work
by a black artist. Another group member iden-
tifies herself as Korean and describes feeling less
aware of her identity in this group than in other
groups. Another member begins to reflect on her
identity as a black woman but is interrupted by
the amplified sound of someone chewing gum.

Four different voices come over the speakers,
overlapping as they read a series of words. They
are periodically interrupted by the sound of a
small crowd responding to a sporting event.

Rich
Selfish
Popular
Stupid
Strong
Curious
Evil
Good
Kind
Poor
Bad
Funny
Clever
Resilient

Intelligent
Mean
Generous
Cunning
Weak

Pretty
Alive
Woman
Citizen
Well
There
Young
Girl
Dead
Sick
Ugly
Man
Old
Alien
Boy
Here

Son
Parent
Wife
Husband
Sister
Brother
Sibling
Spouse
Partner
Girlfriend
Boyfriend
Father
Daughter
Mother
Child
Baby
Aunt
Uncle

BLOOD
BRAIN
MUSCLE
BREATH
BONES
PISS

Toe
Toenail
Lips
Hand
Body

Head
Teeth
Eyes
Nose
Mouth
Hair
Ear
Tooth
Nostril
Earlobe
Jaw
Neck
Tongue
Face
Chest
Brow
Forehead
Nape
Breast
Nipple
Shoulder
Arm
Elbow
Wrist
Thumb
Finger
Fingernail
Pinky
Palm
Armpit
Back
Ass
Leg
Knee
Abdomen
Vagina
Cheek
Ankle
Penis
Foot

Audio: synth organ music.

Ninety minutes have elapsed since I introduced the group process. The group disperses. People get their coats.

Audio: the artist howling and whimpering along with a dog, followed by the voice of Toni Morrison reading a passage from Sula.

While in this state of weary anticipation she noticed that she was not breathing, that her heart had stopped completely. A crease of fear touched her breast, for any second there was sure to be a violent explosion in her brain, a gasping for breath. Then she realized, or rather, she sensed, that there was not going to be any pain. She was not breathing because she didn't have to. Her body did not need oxygen. She was dead. Sula felt her face smiling. "Well, I'll be damned," she thought, "it didn't even hurt. Wait'll I tell Nel."[4]

As we file out of the gallery onto the street, the sound of paramedic personnel speaking over an emergency radio system plays over the speakers followed by the sounds of polyphonic synthesizer music and coughing at random moments—the same audio that played as the gathering began.

Notes

1 Nikita Gale, "Slow Ruin," *Text zur Kunst* (August 26, 2020), https://www.textezurkunst.de/articles/nikita-gale-slow-ruin/.

2 Gale also explains that, in addition to being an artist, I trained as a group-relations consultant and developed an application of group relations to engage with art as a group, which the artist experienced as my student at the University of California, Los Angeles.

3 Participants included Michaela Bathrick, Ohan Breiding, Abigail Collins, Catharine Czudej, veronique d'entremont, Malik Gaines, Ebony L. Haynes, John Hulsey, Adela Kim, Alyssa Mattocks, Alexander Provan, Ellie Rines, Alan Ruiz, and Alexandro Segade.

4 Toni Morrison, *Sula* (New York: Alfred A. Knopf, 2002), p. 149.

PLATES

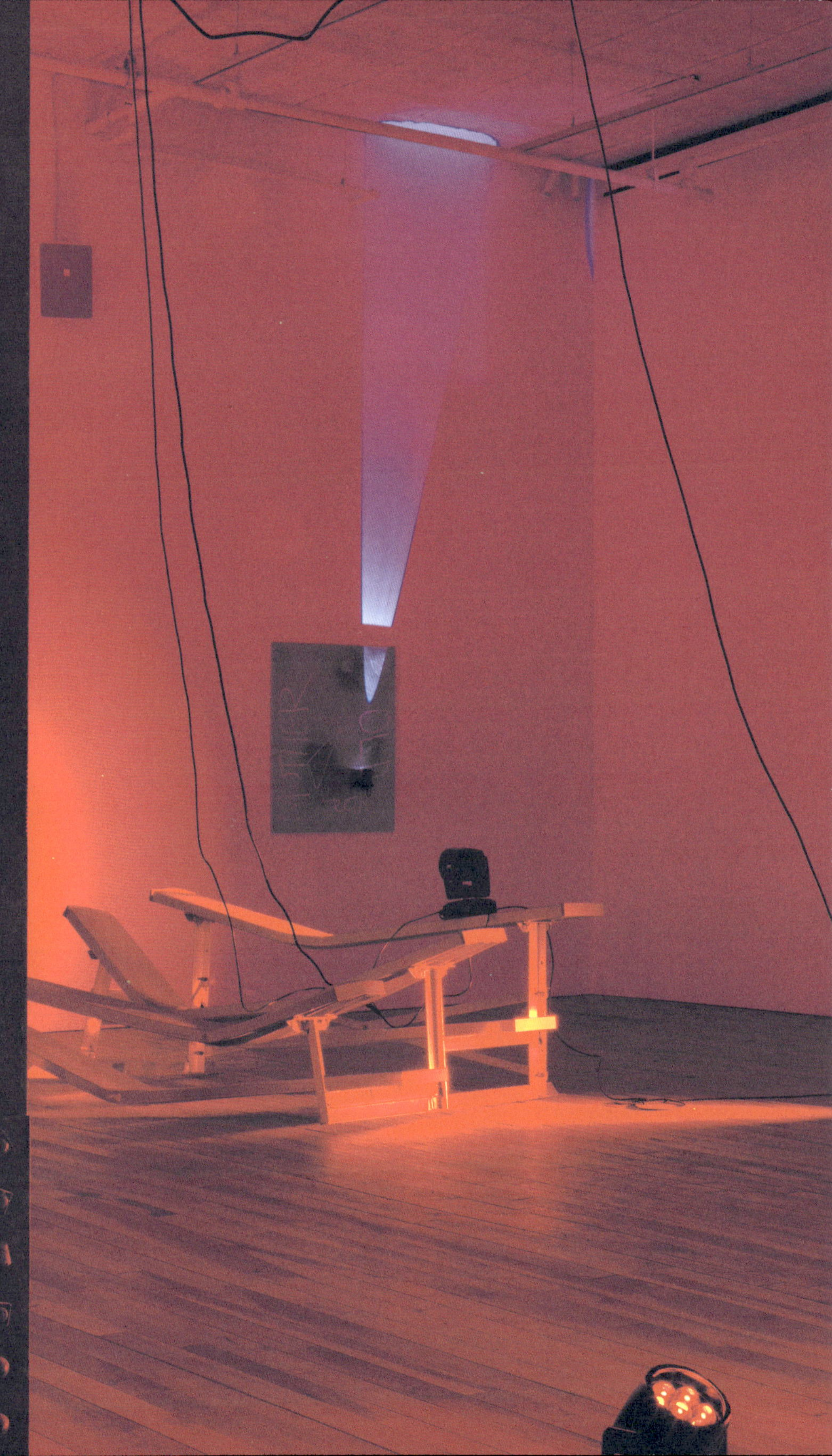

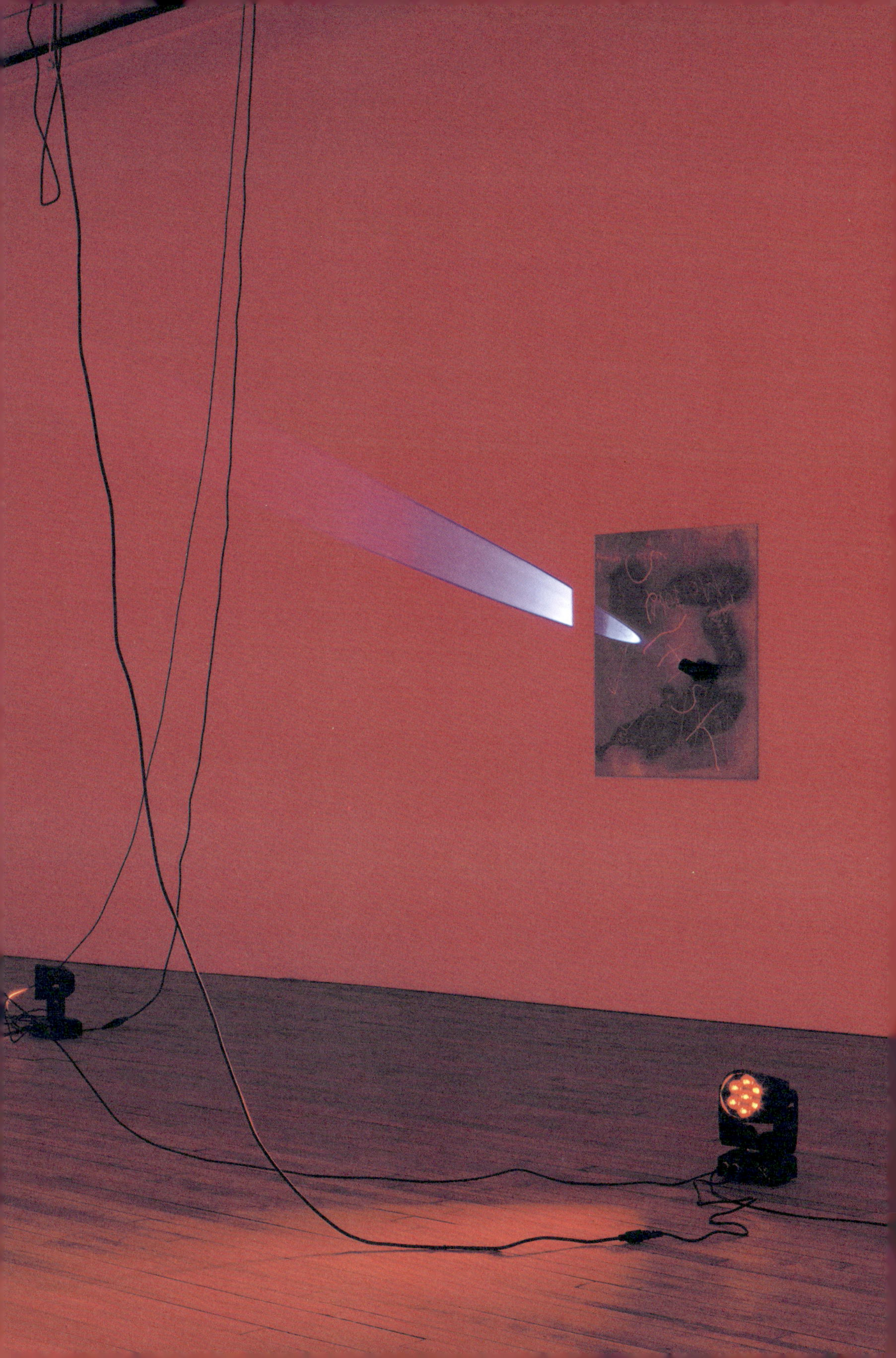

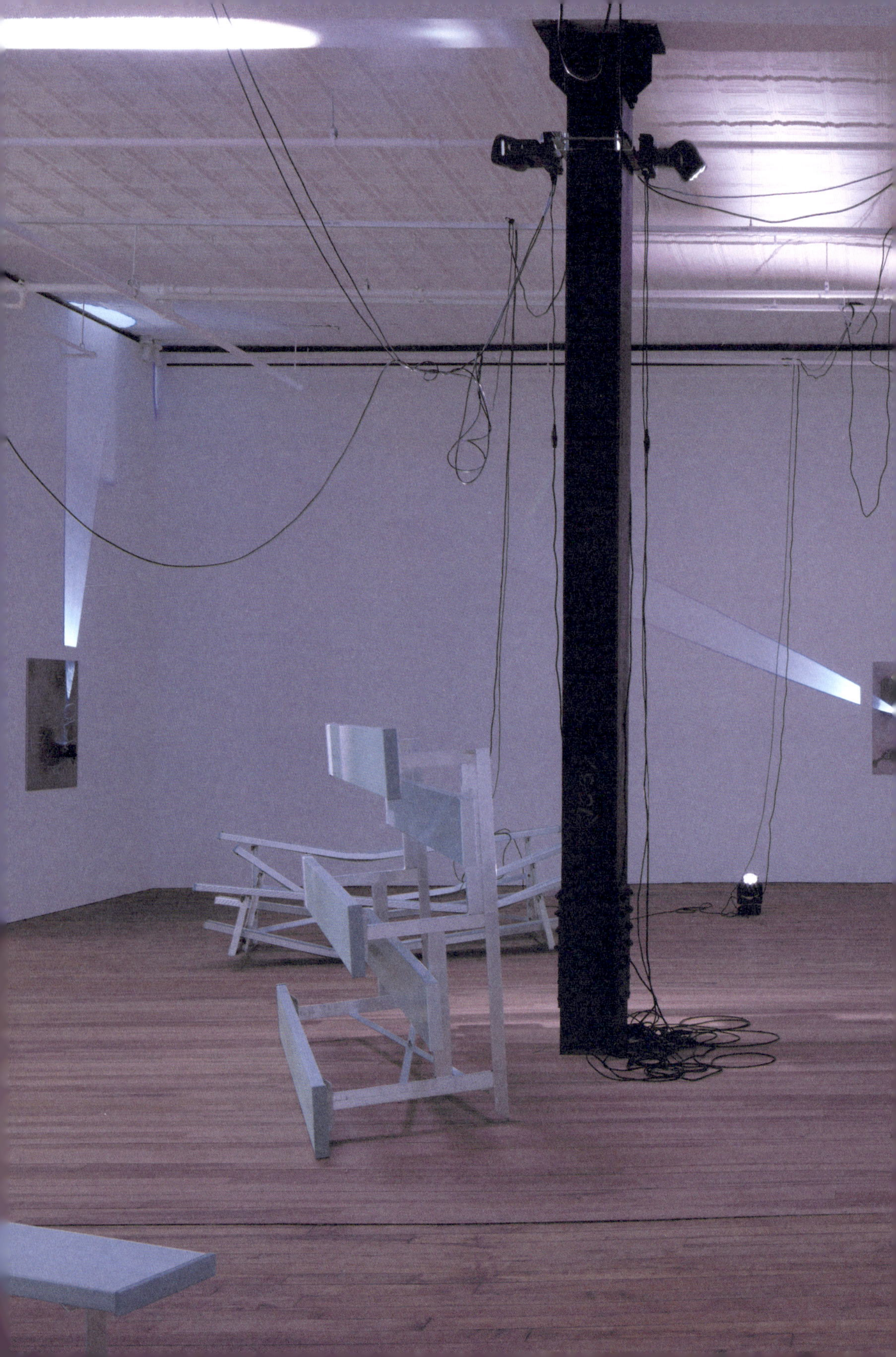

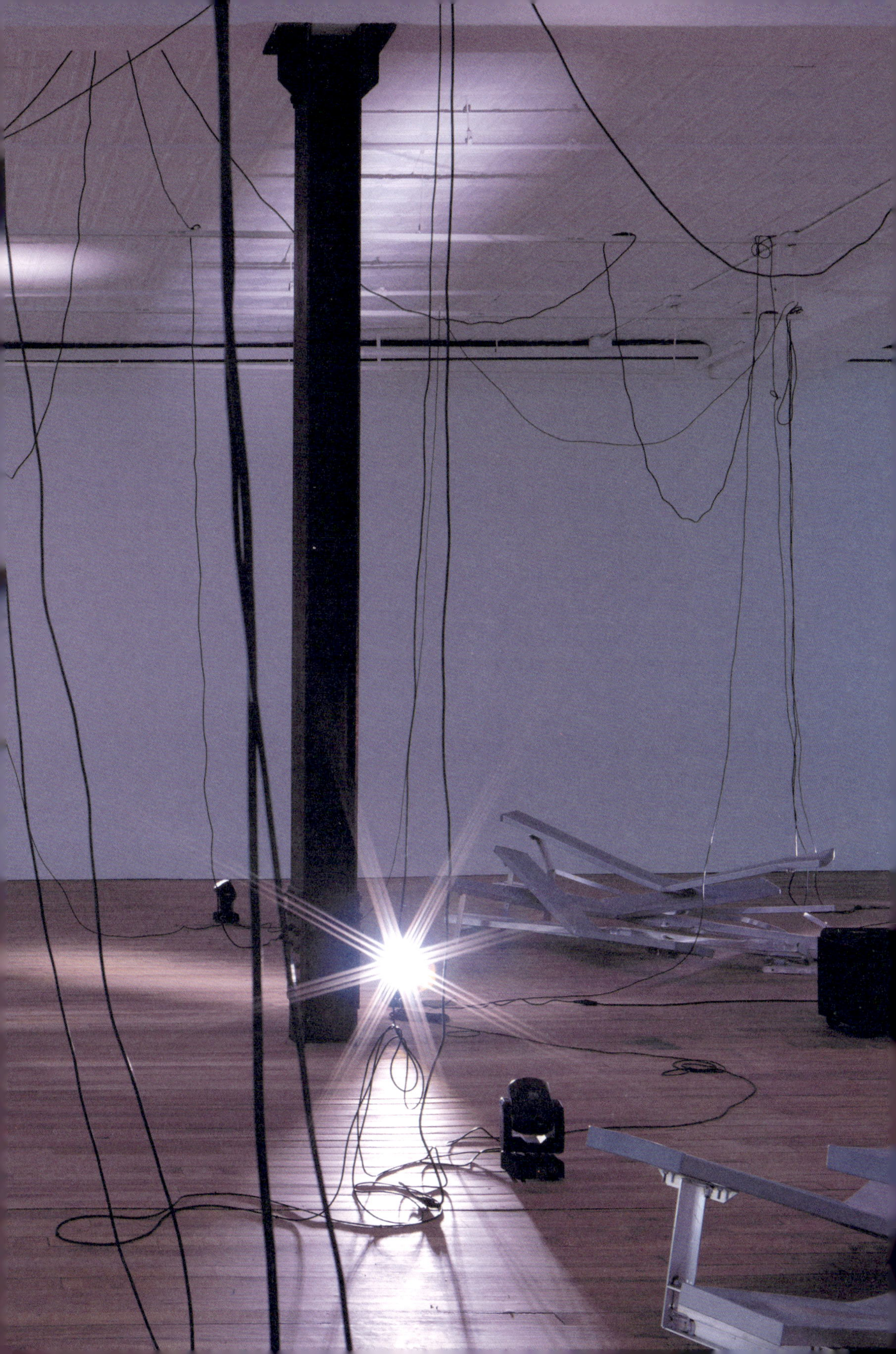

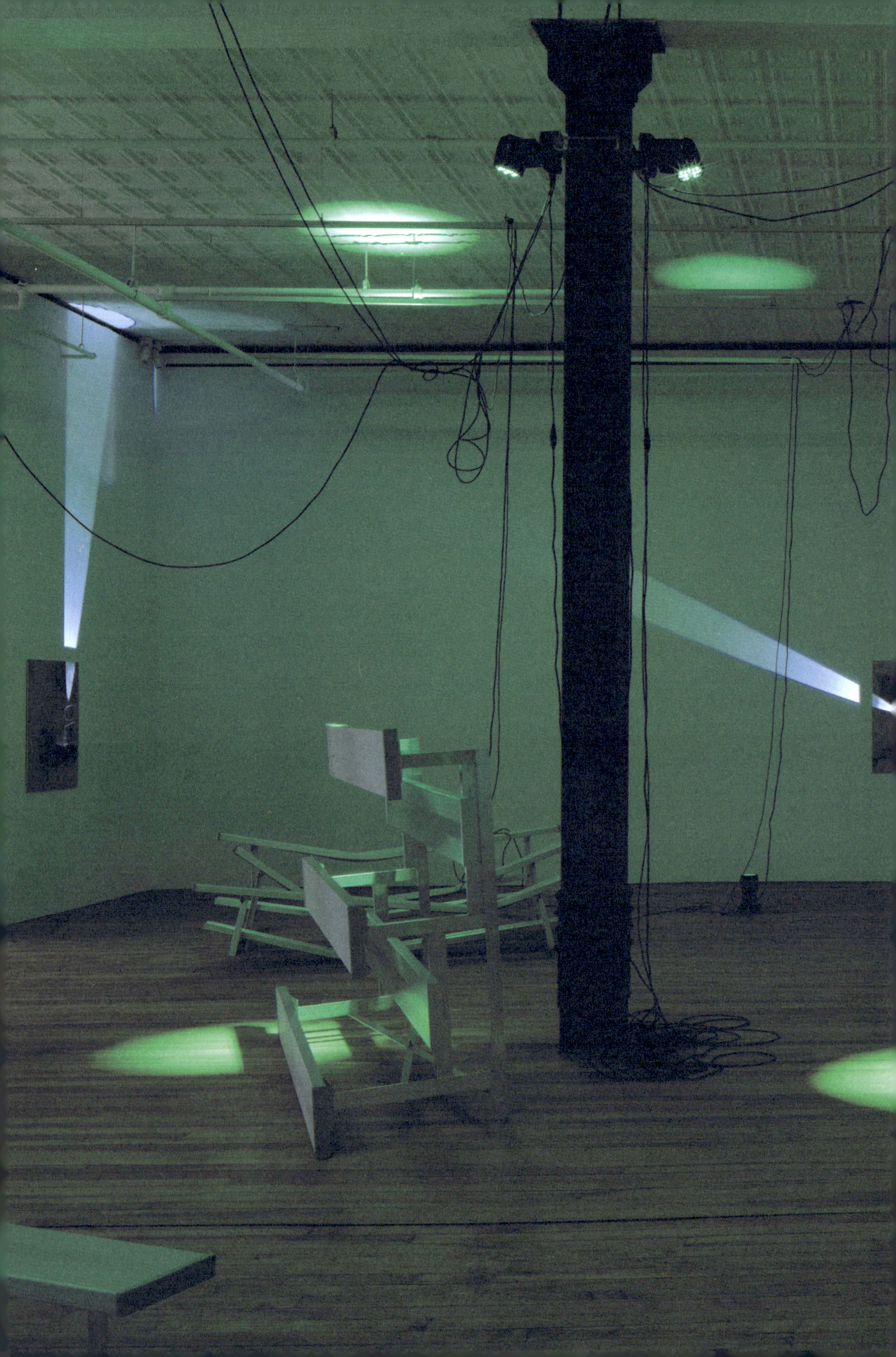

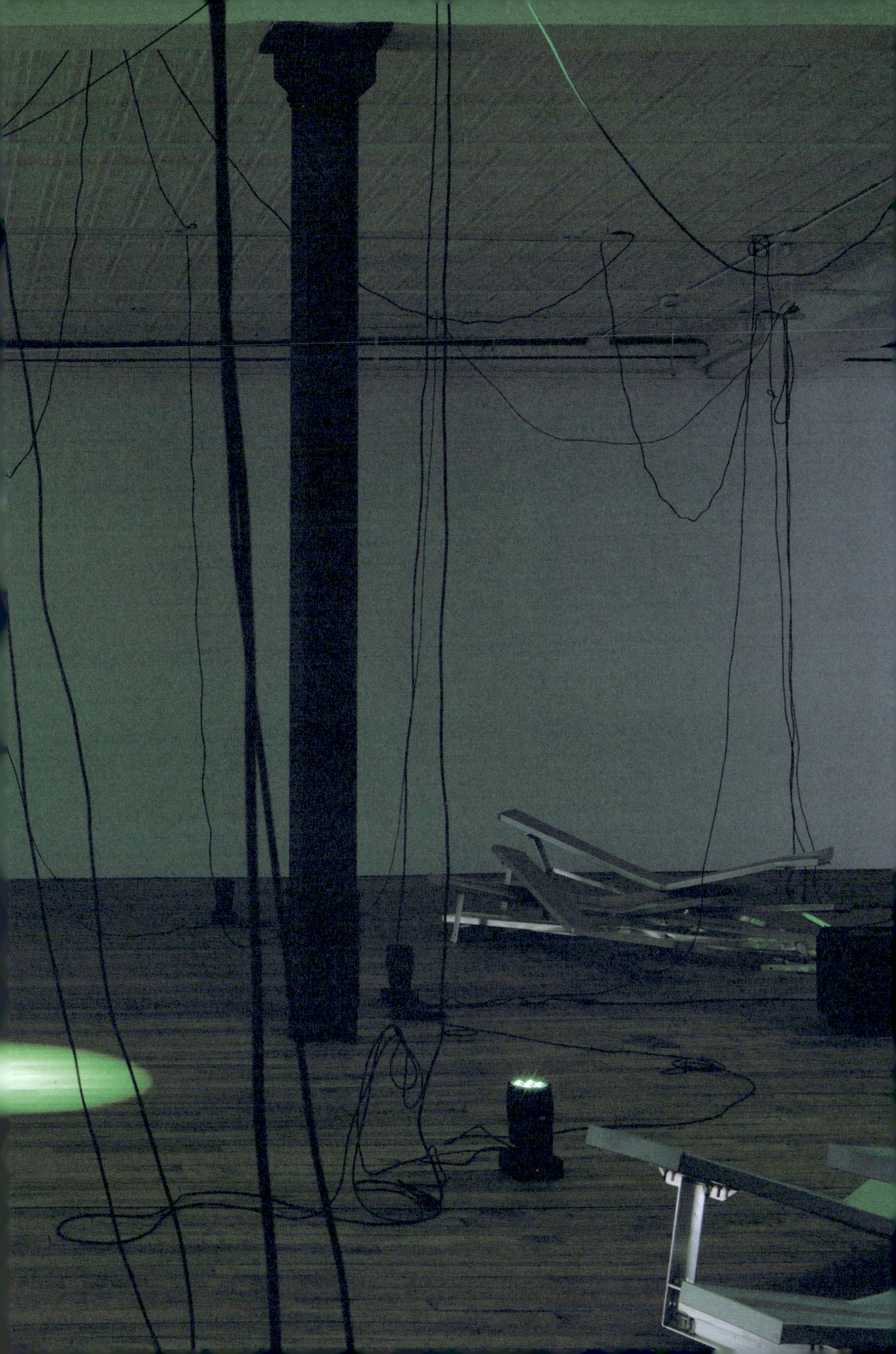

All installation views:
END OF SUBJECT, 2022
Six aluminum bleachers, automated lighting system, four-channel sound
Dimensions variable

Opposite:
BODY PRINT: BONES, 2022
Stain, etching, and LED spotlight on aluminum panel
40 × 30 × 4 ½ inches | 101.6 × 76.2 × 11.4 cm

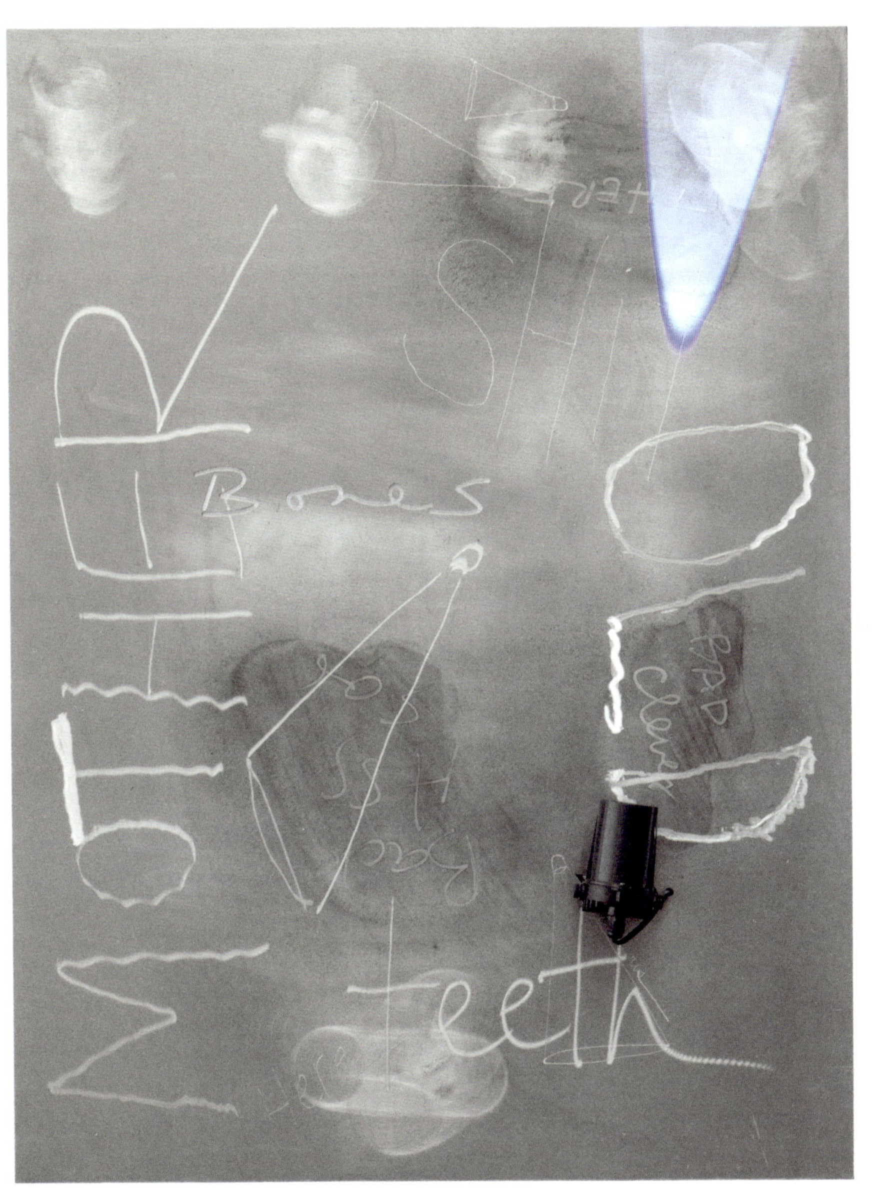

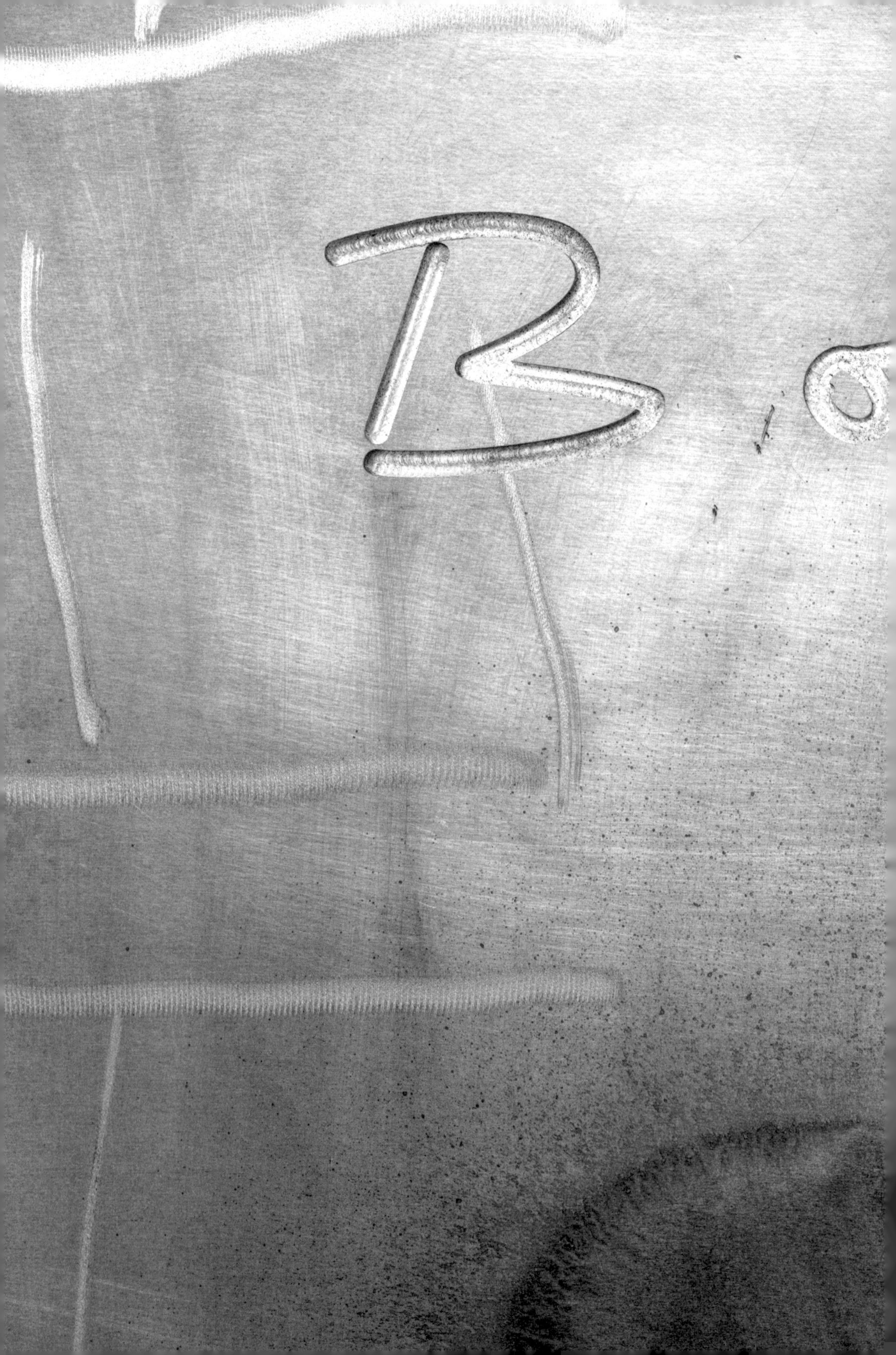

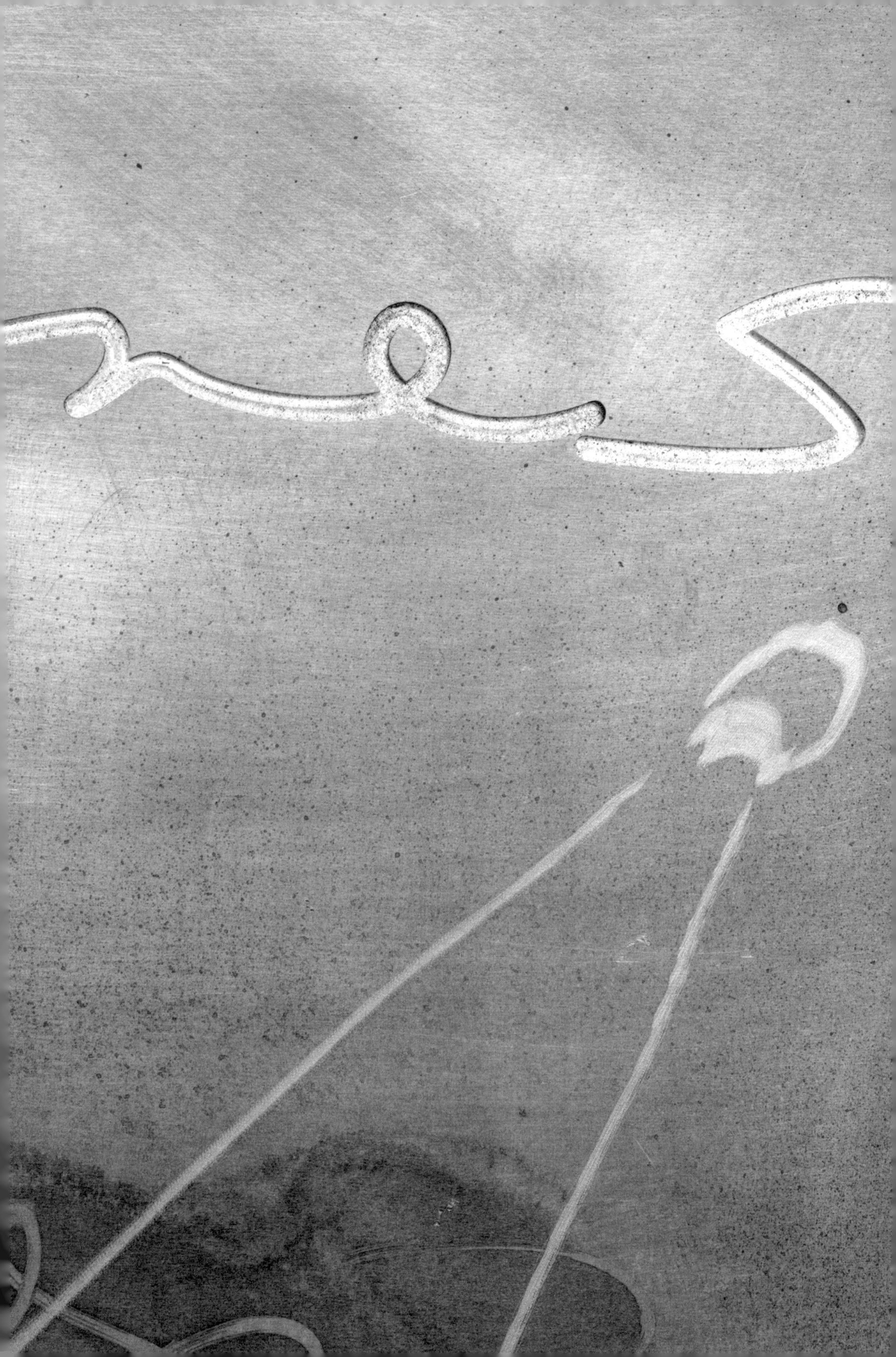

BODY PRINT: PISS, 2022
Stain, etching, and LED spotlight on aluminum panel
40 × 30 × 4 ½ inches | 101.6 × 76.2 × 11.4 cm

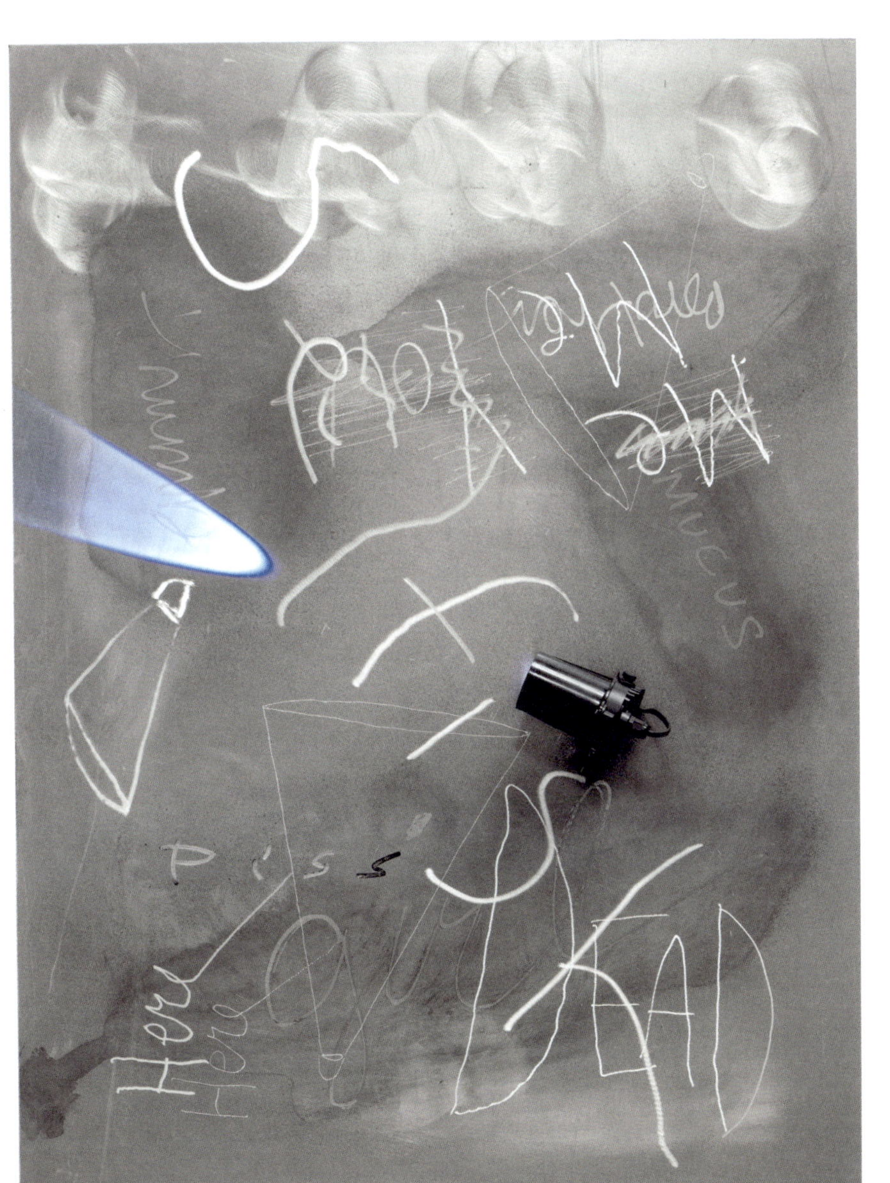

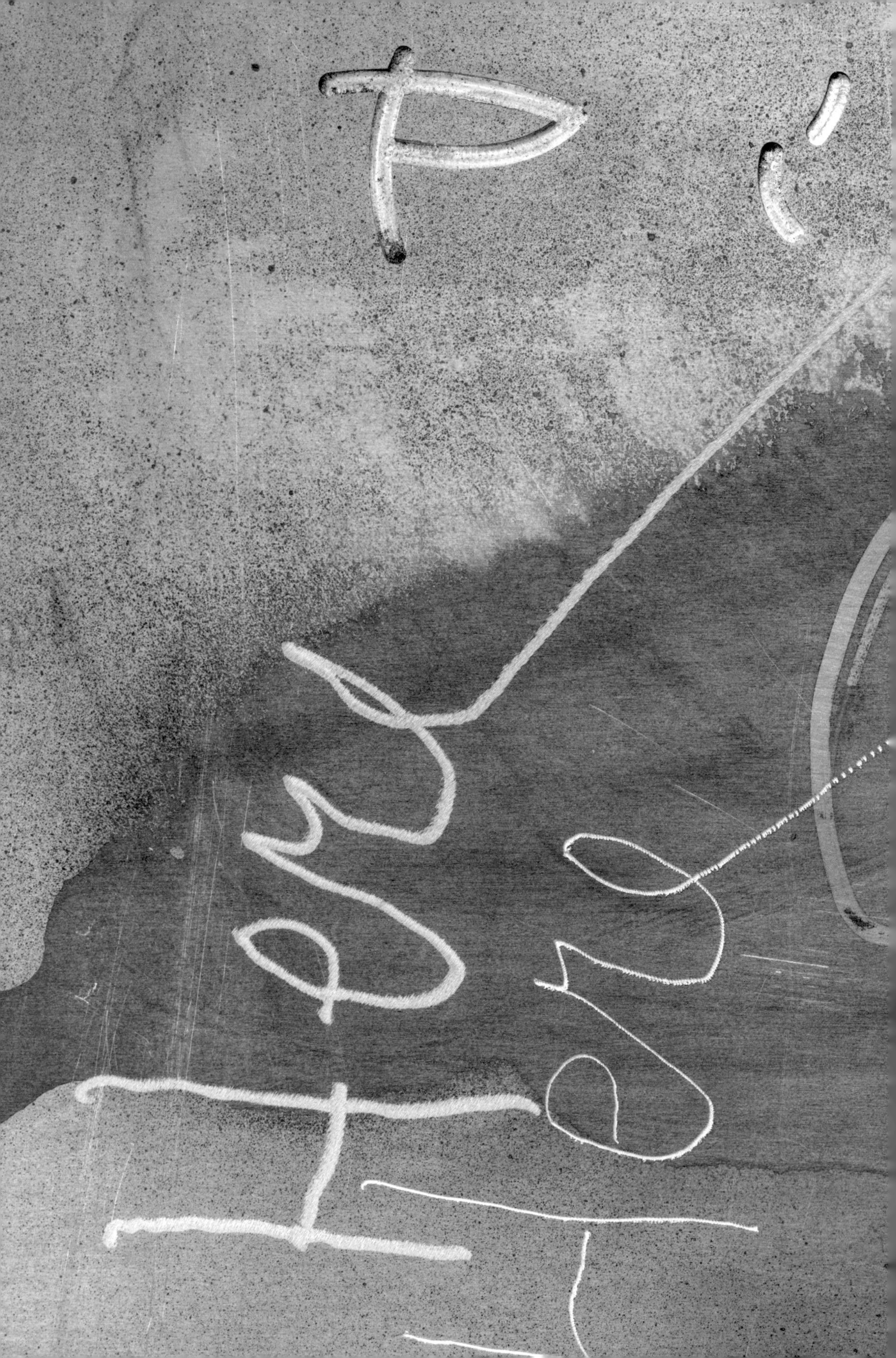

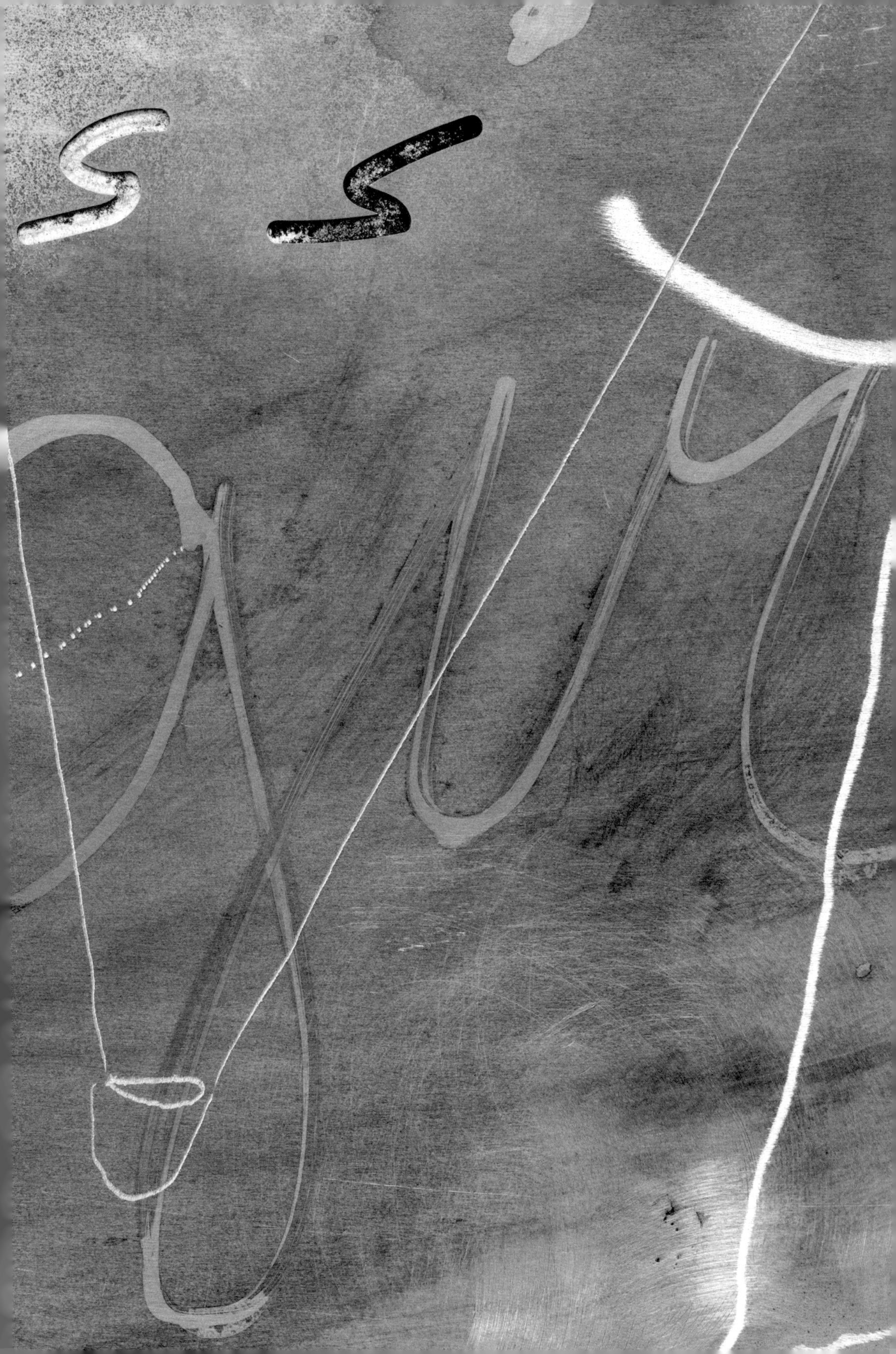

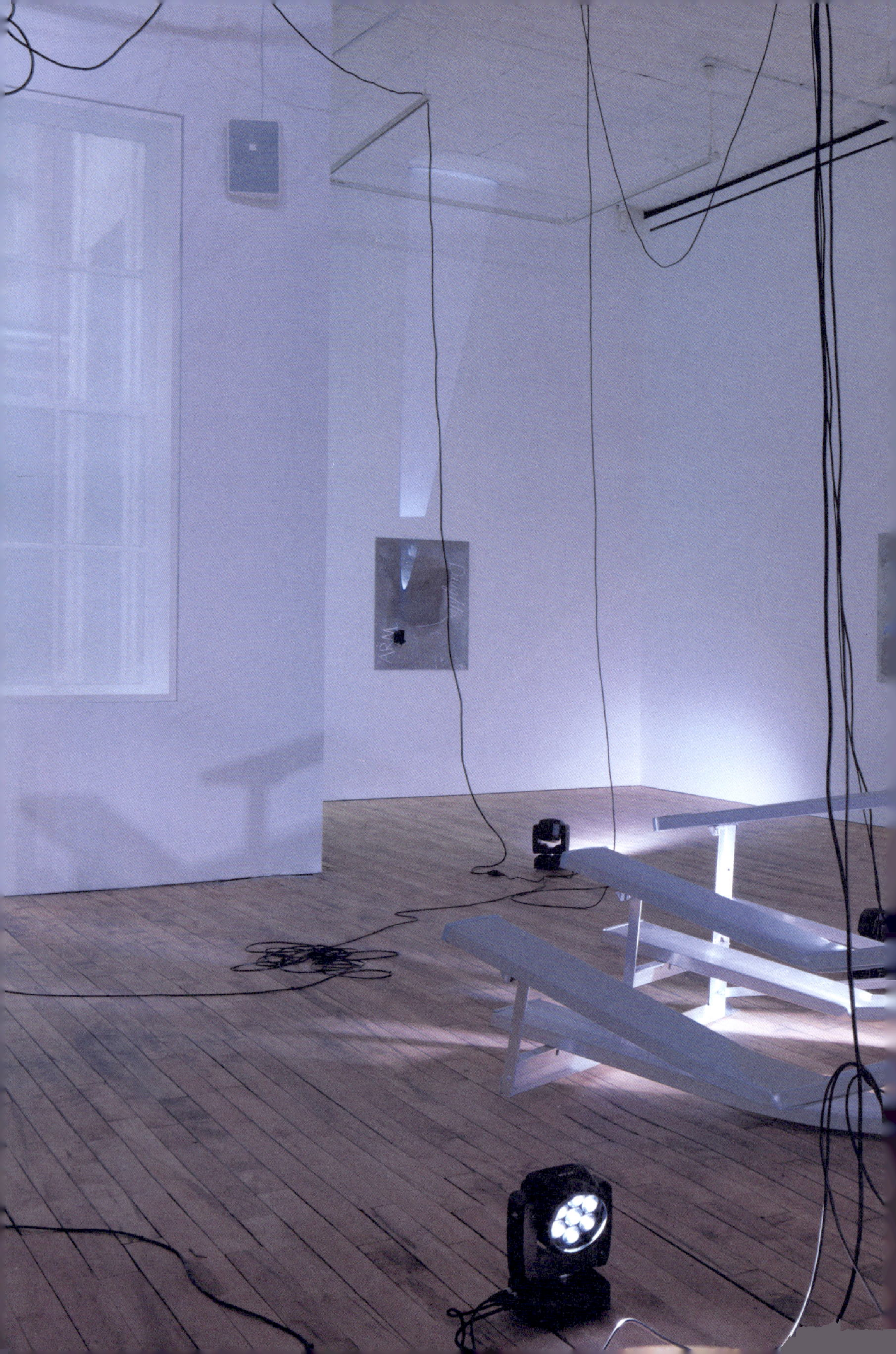

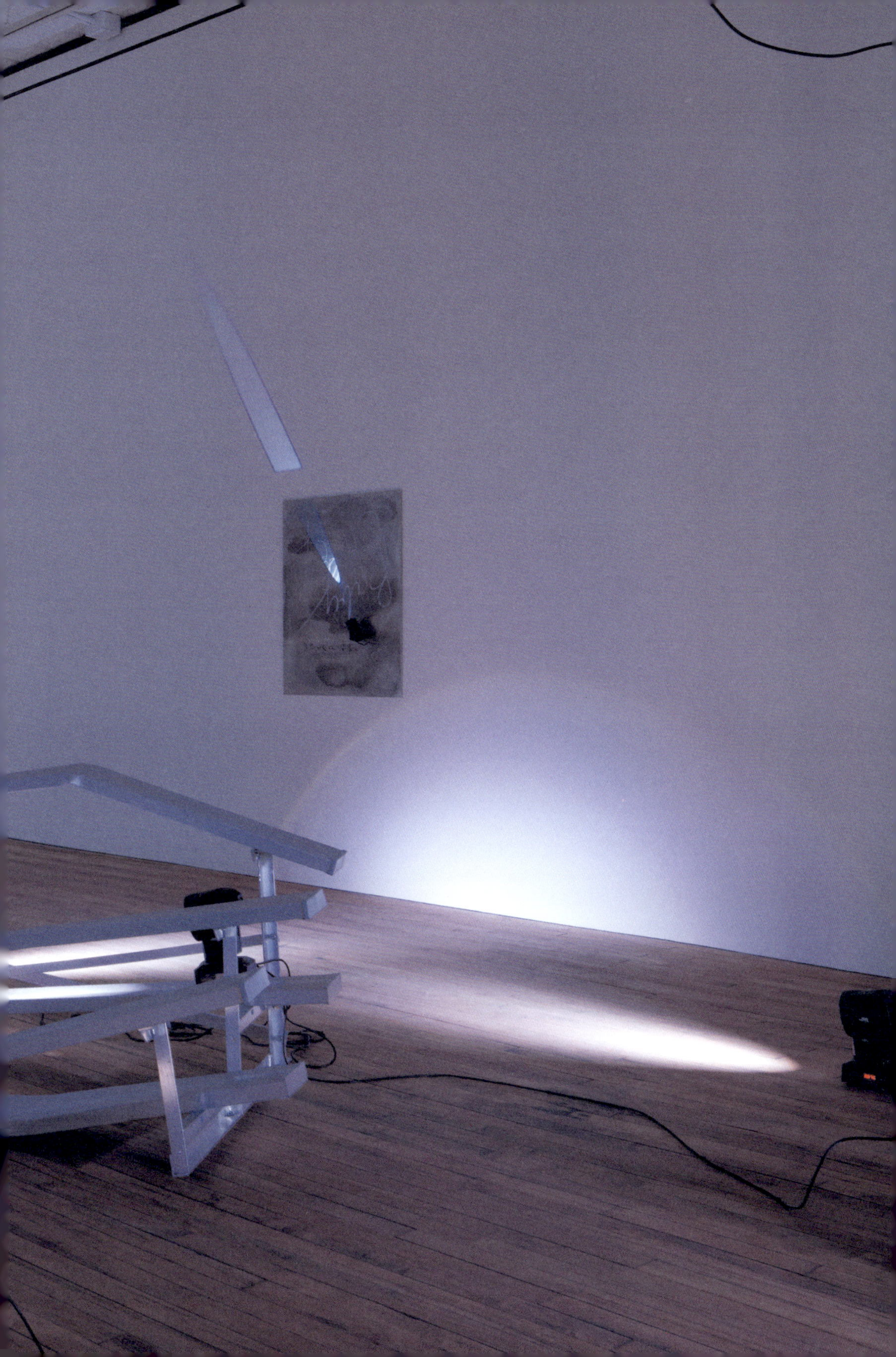

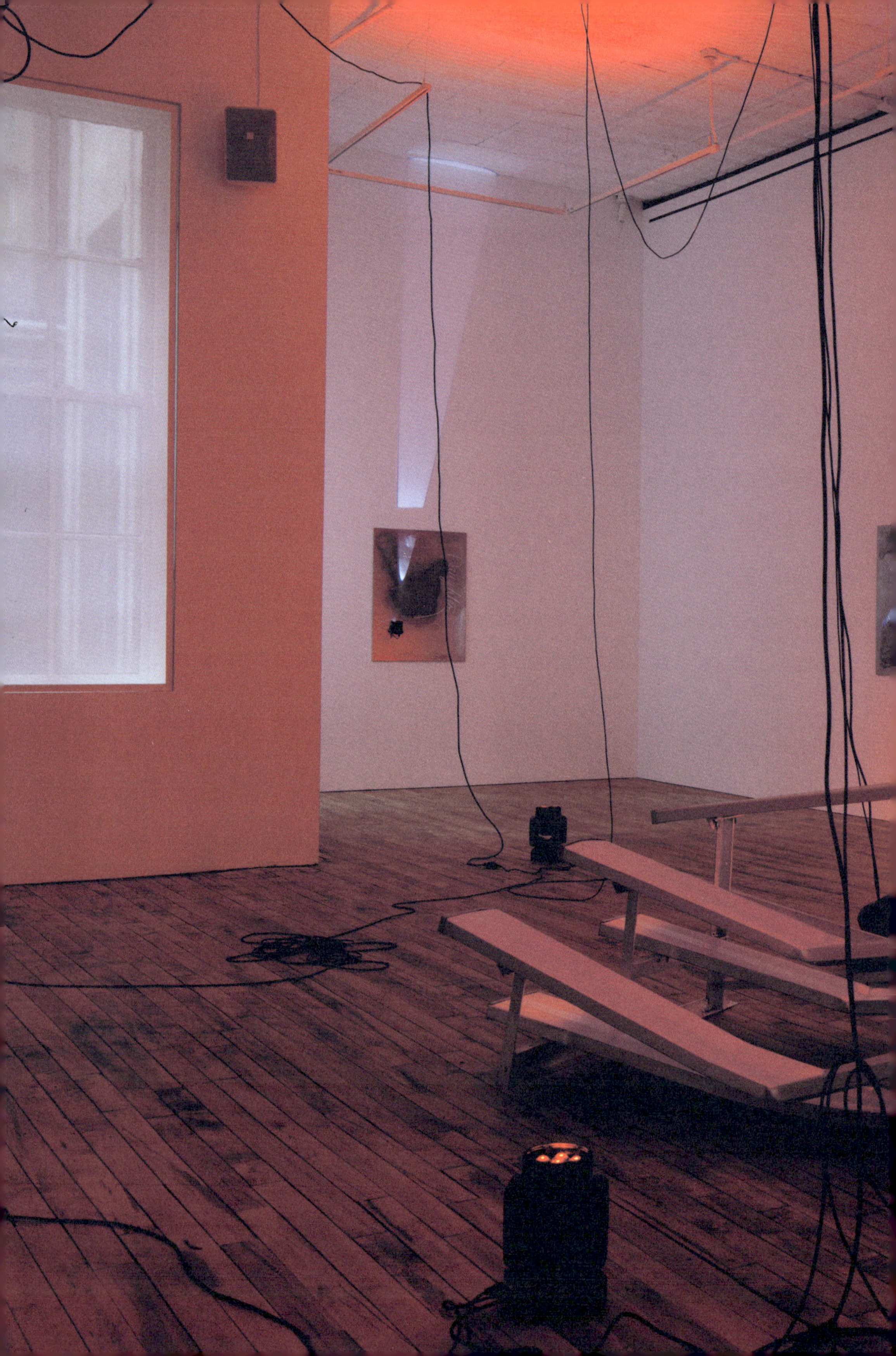

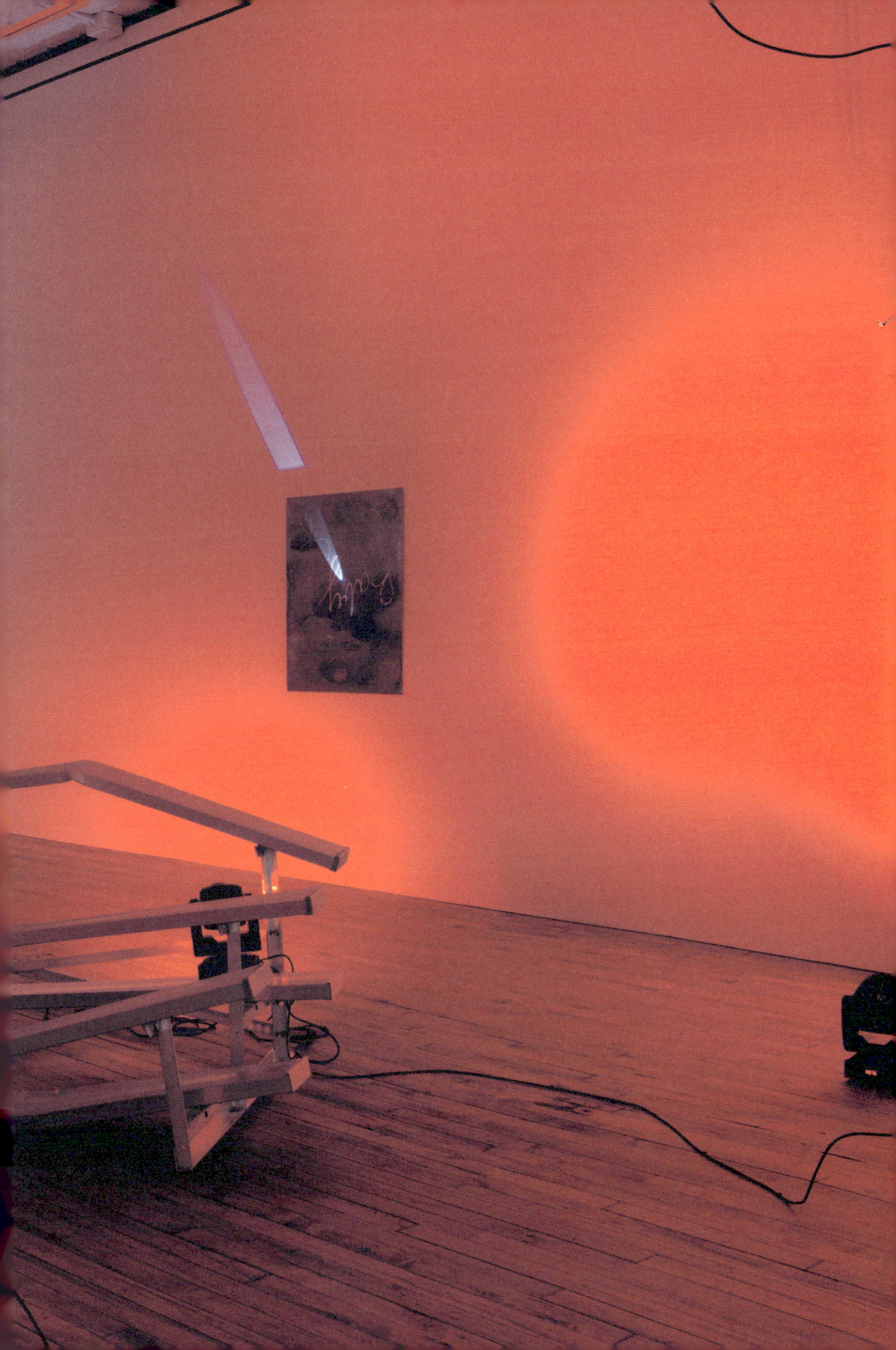

BODY PRINT: MUSCLE, 2022
Stain, etching, and LED spotlight on aluminum panel
40 × 30 × 4 ½ inches | 101.6 × 76.2 × 11.4 cm

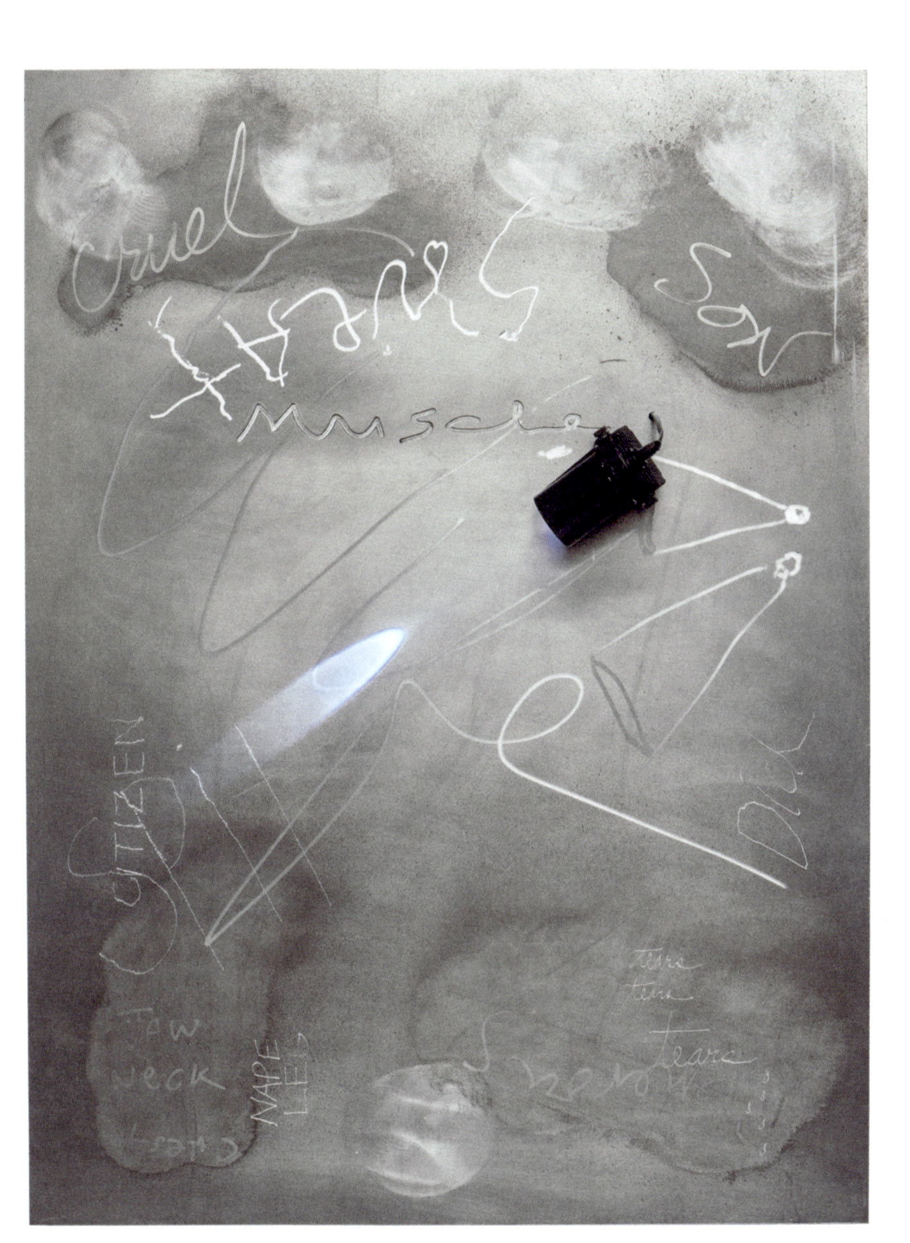

cruel
sweat
muscle
son
CITIZEN
NAPE
LIP
low
neck
tears
tears
tears

tears

tears

tears

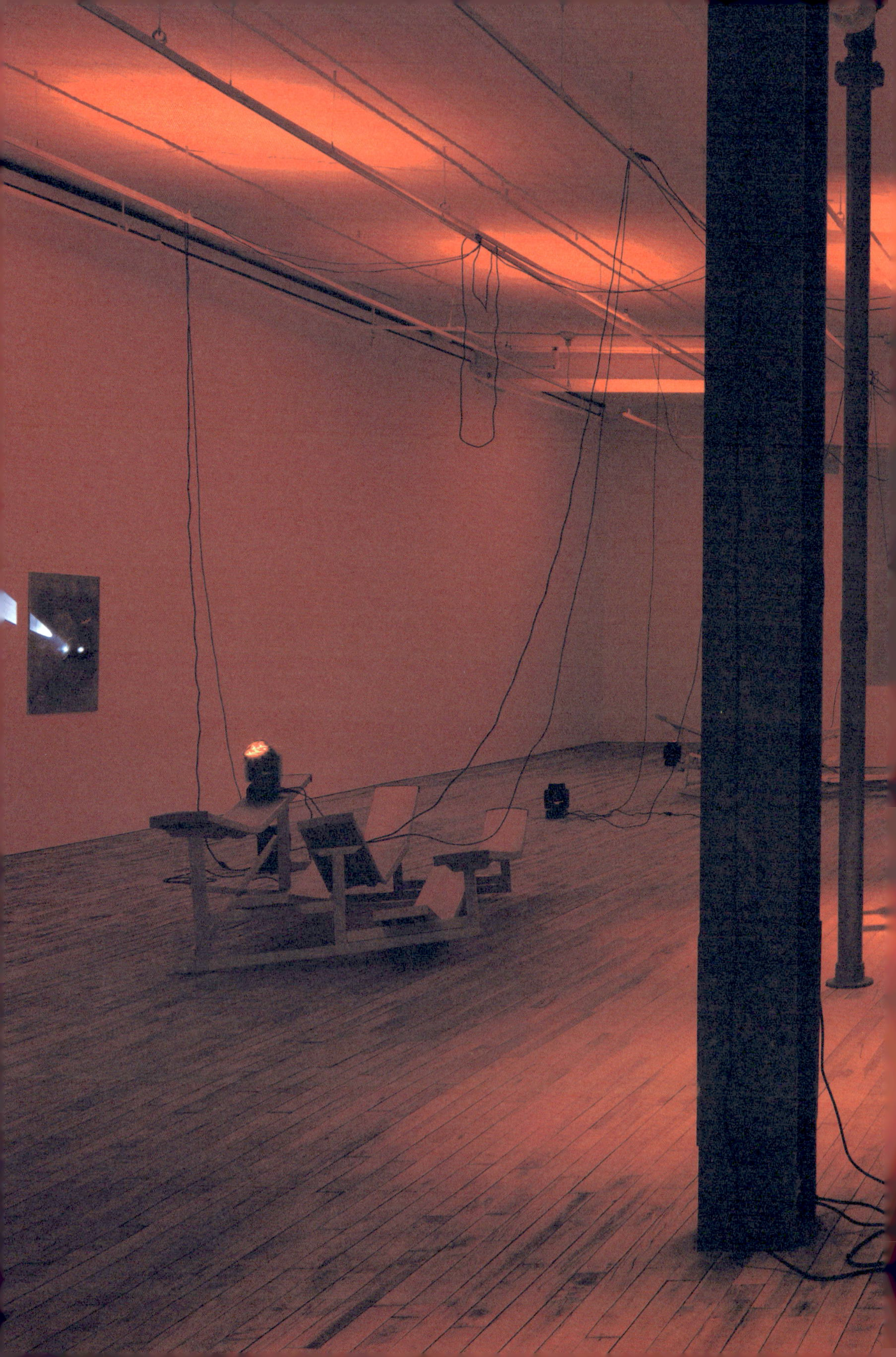

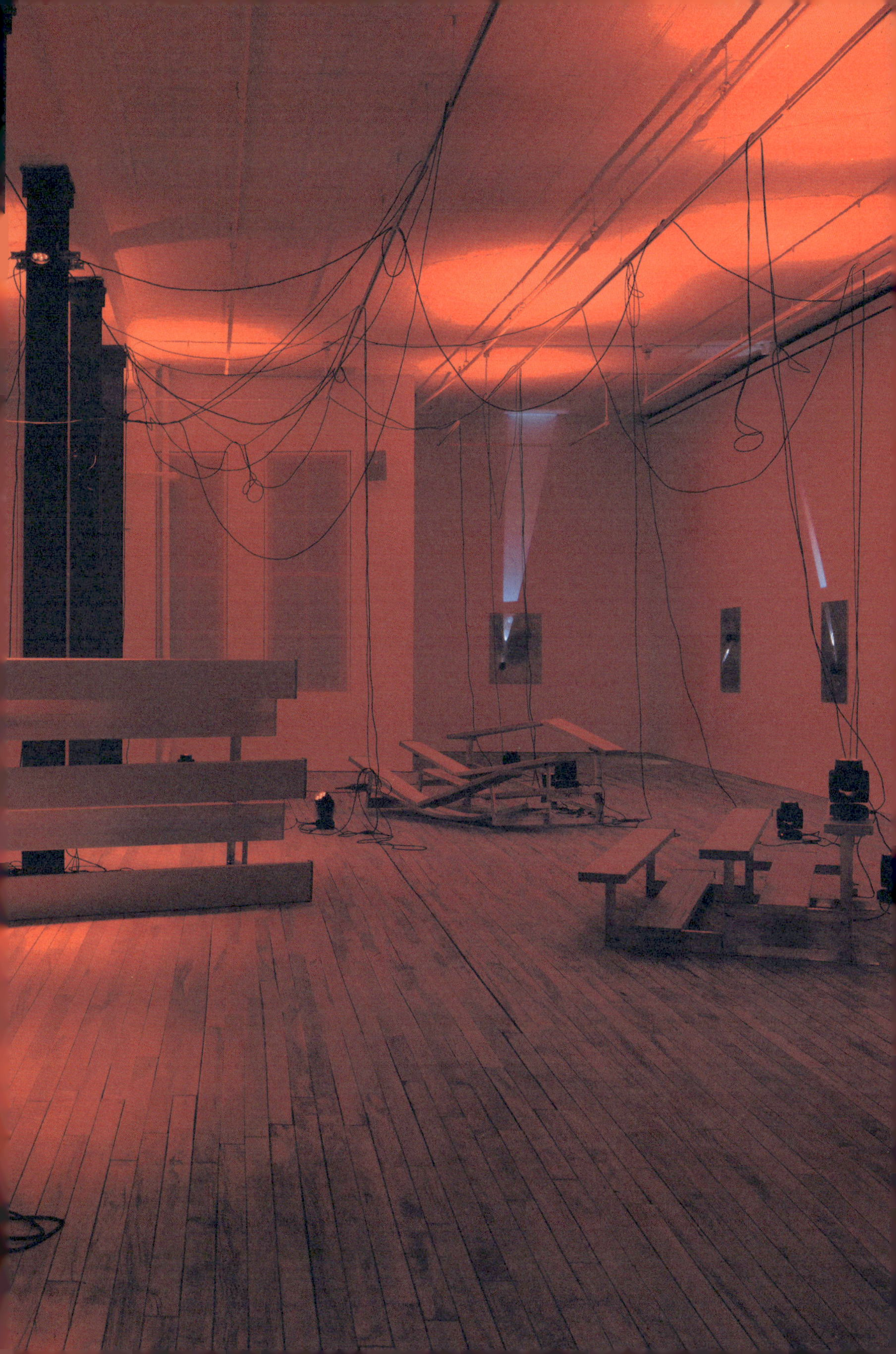

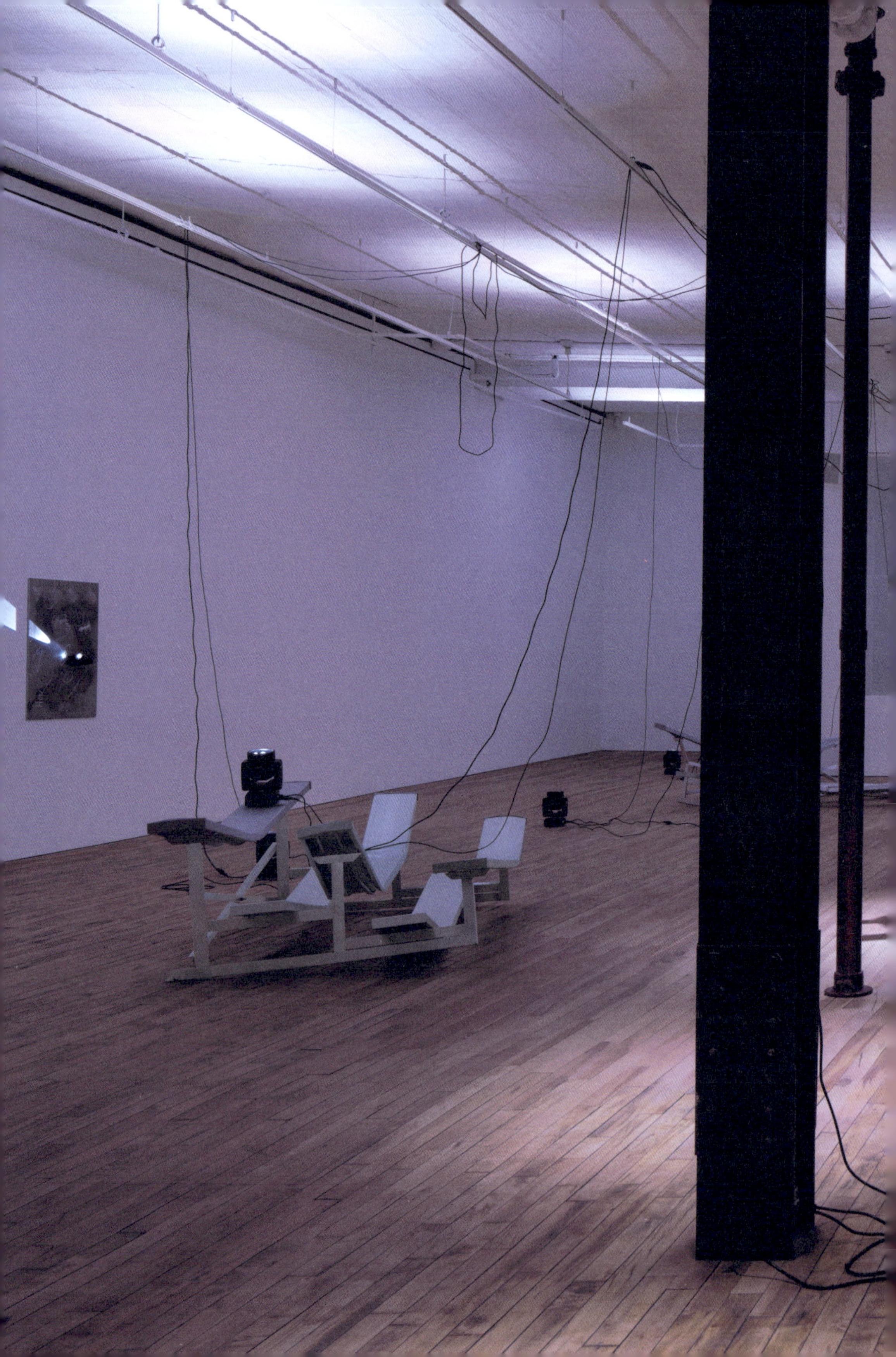

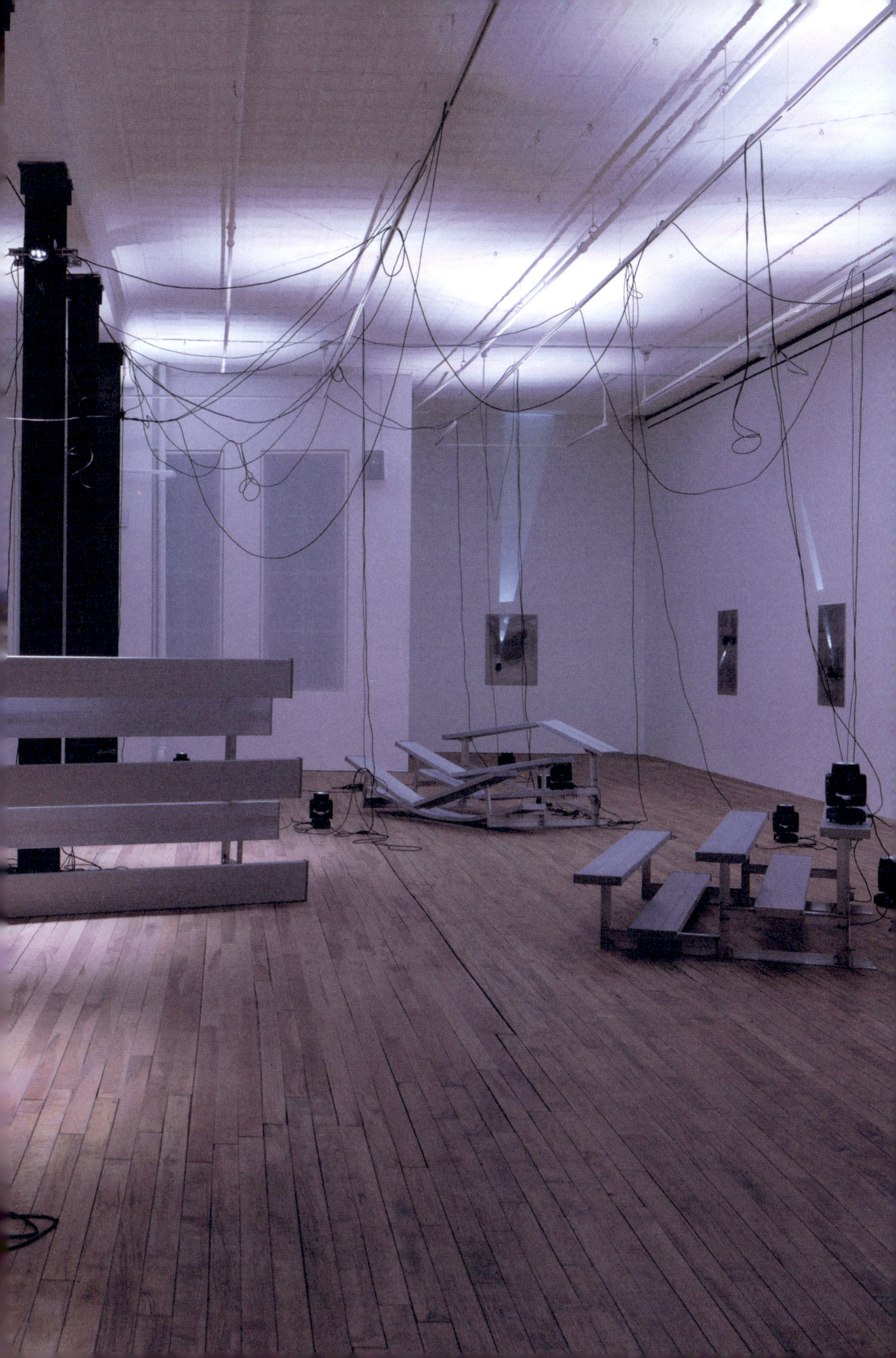

BODY PRINT: BREATH, 2022
Stain, etching, and LED spotlight on aluminum panel
40 × 30 × 4 ½ inches | 101.6 × 76.2 × 11.4 cm

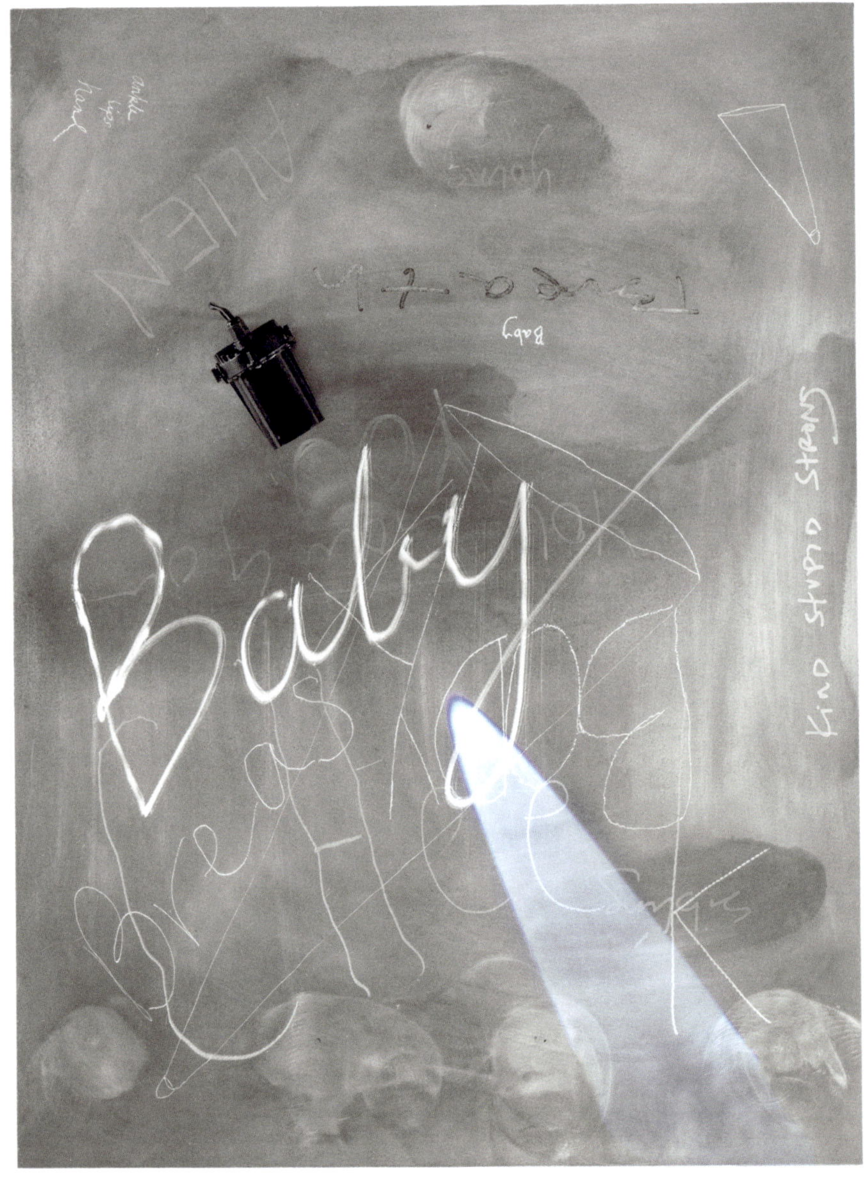
Baby
breath
ALIEN
Baby
KiND stvPiD stvPiD

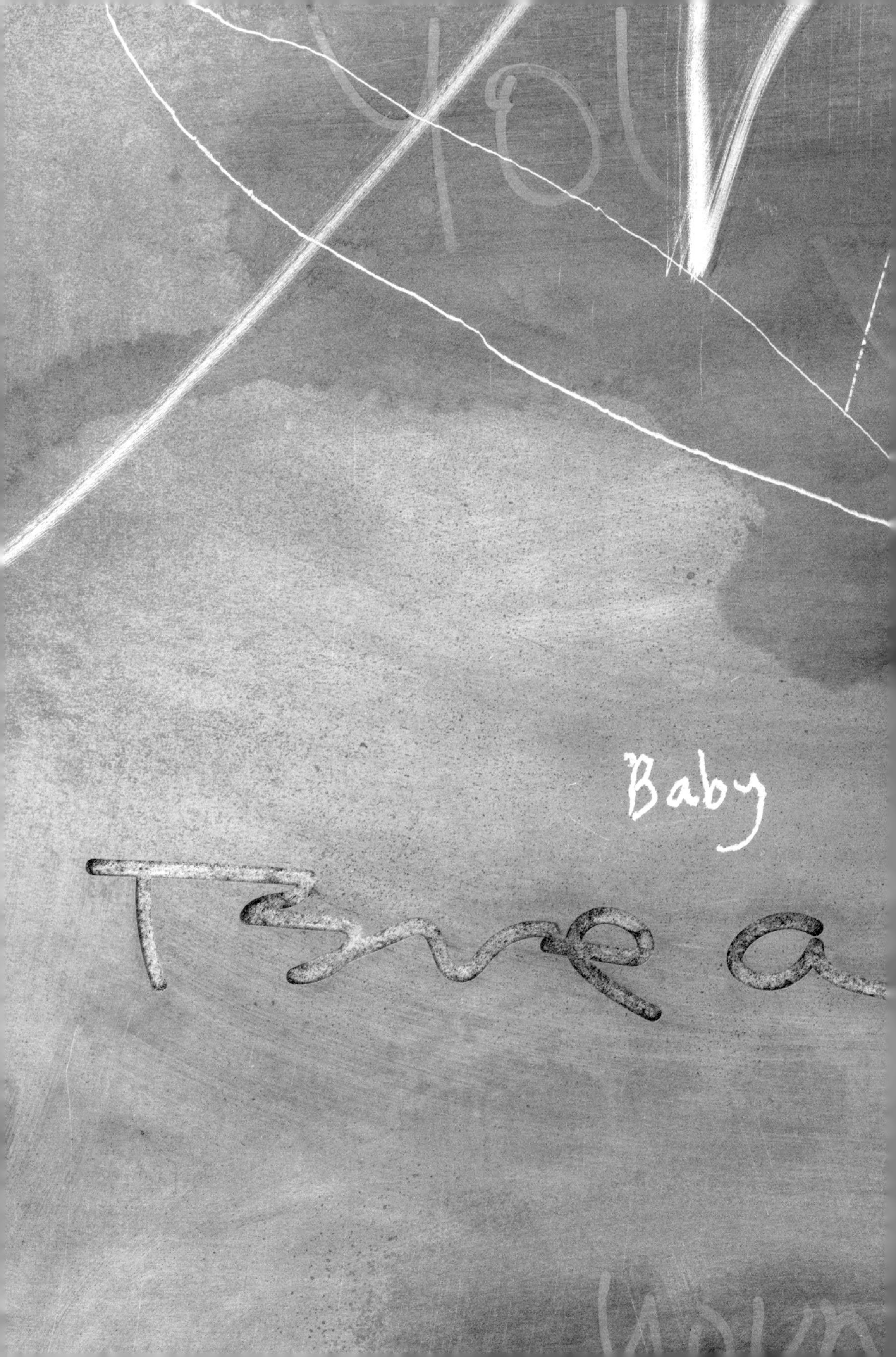
Baby

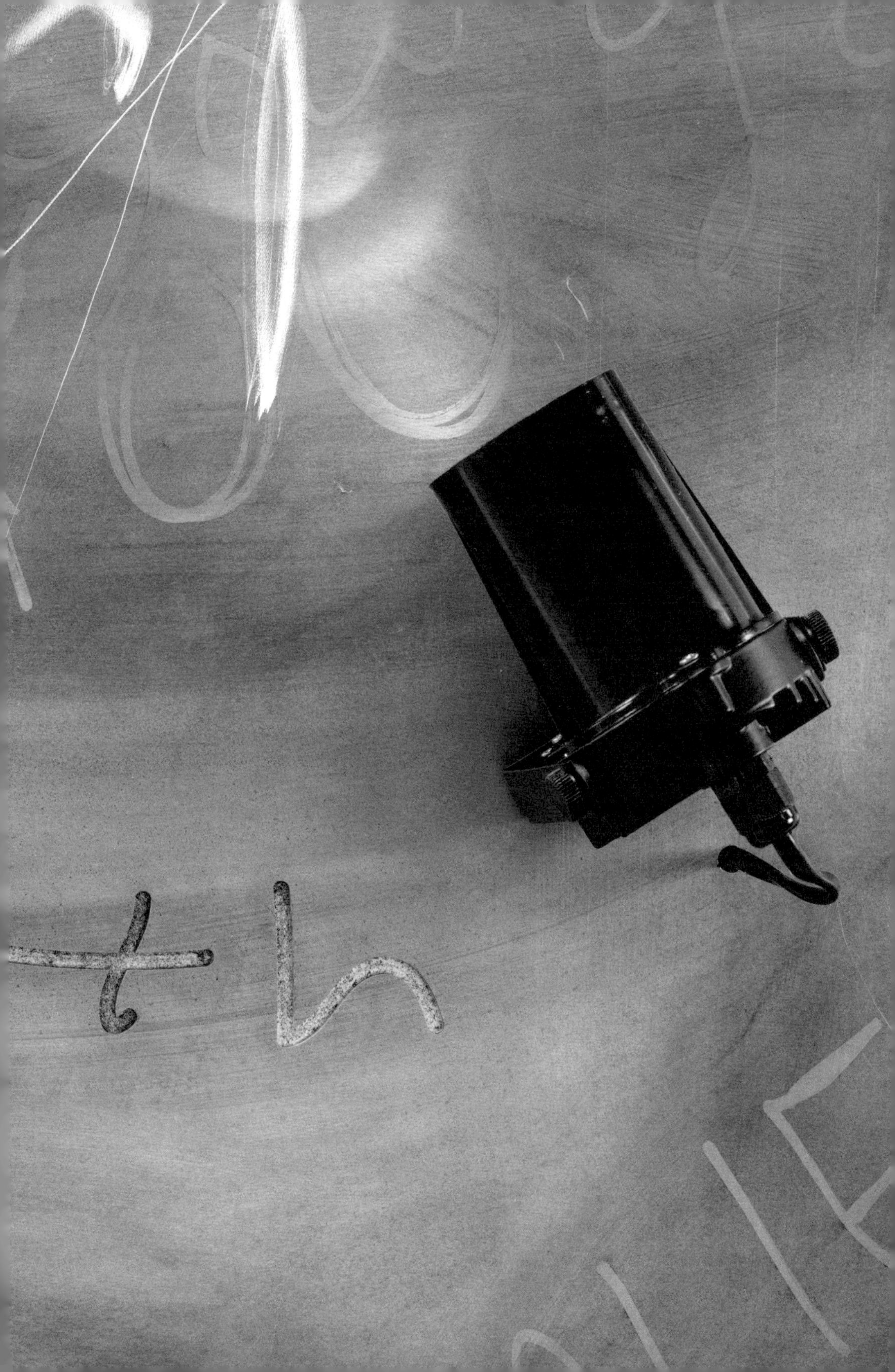

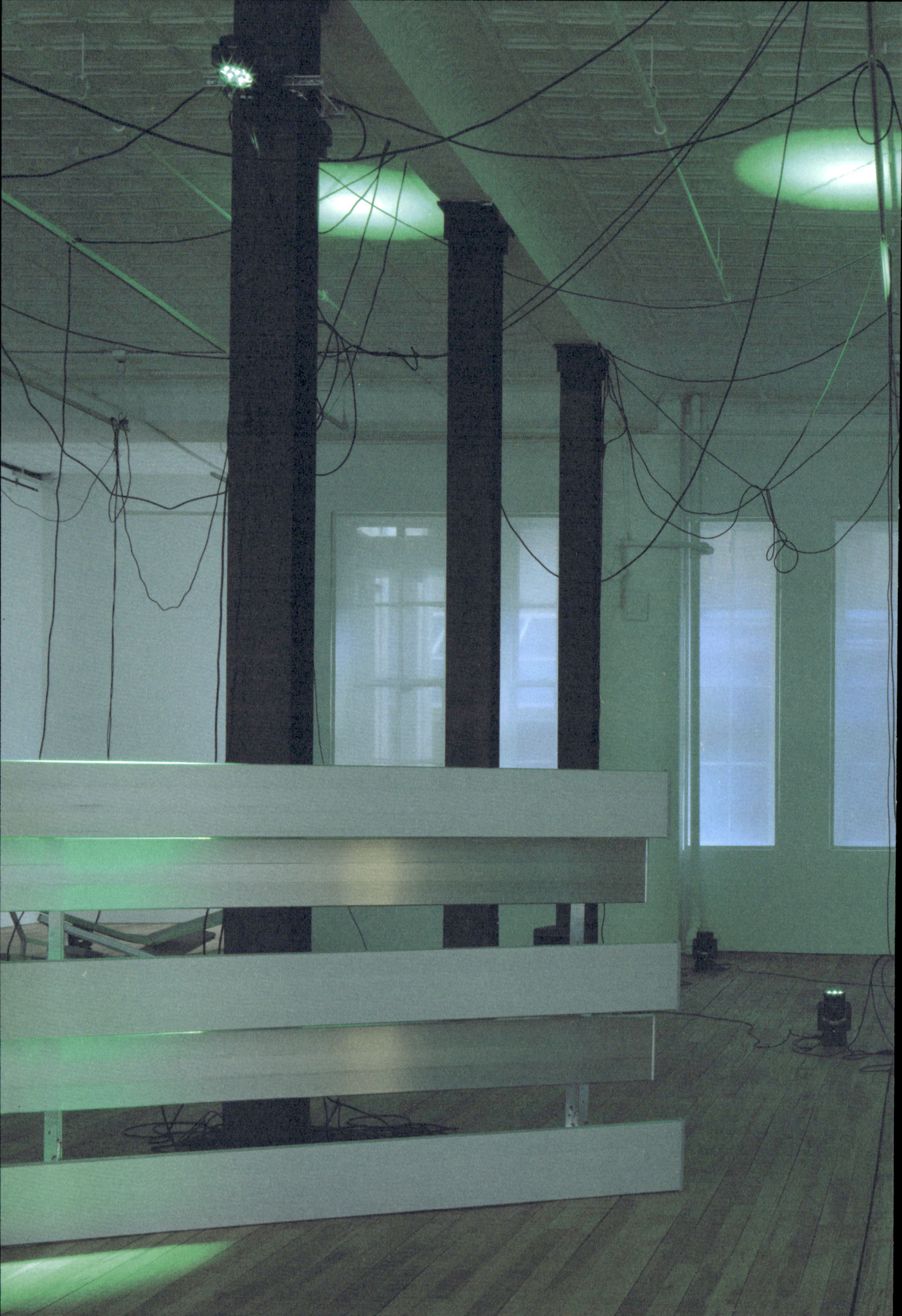

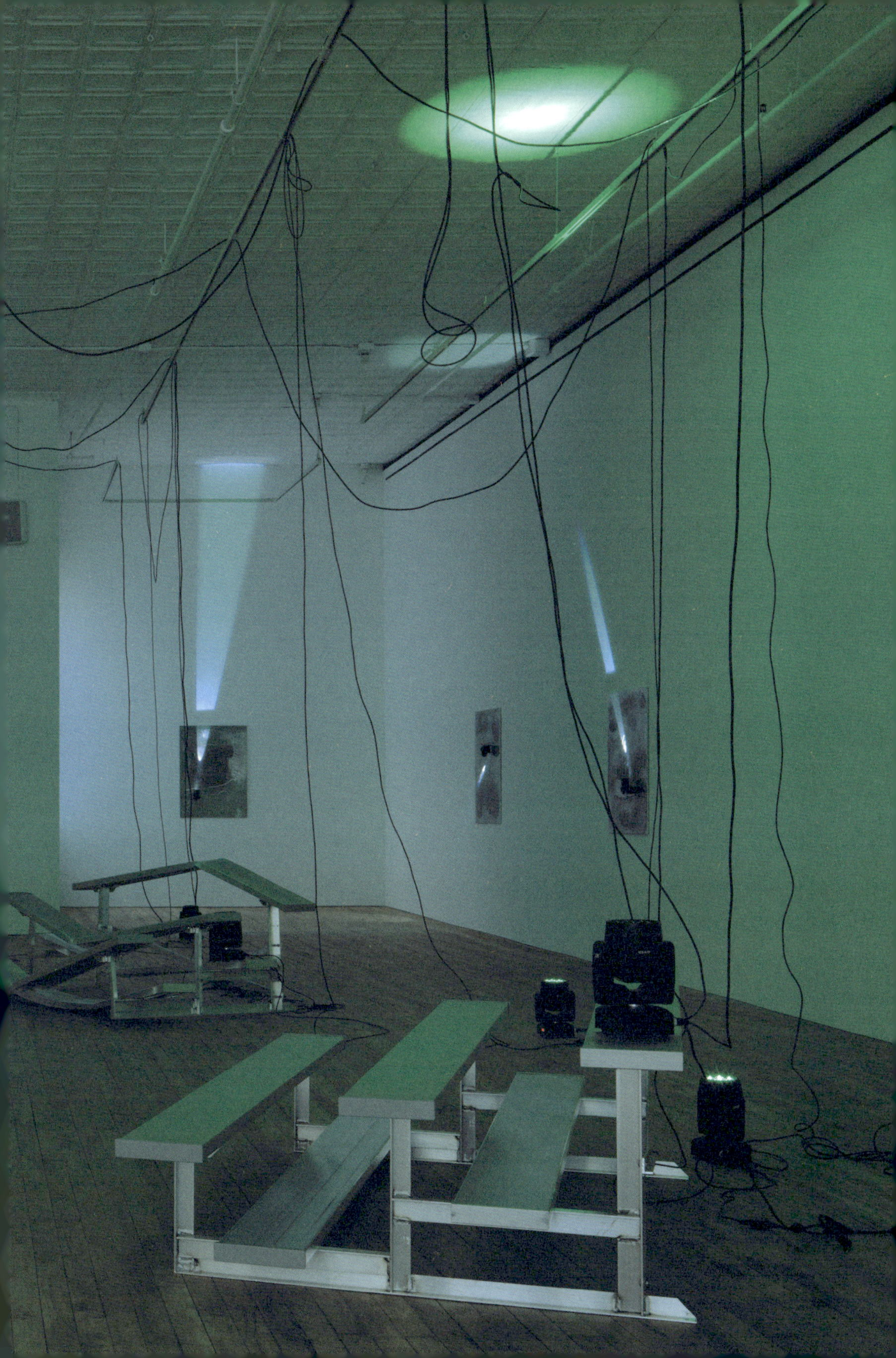

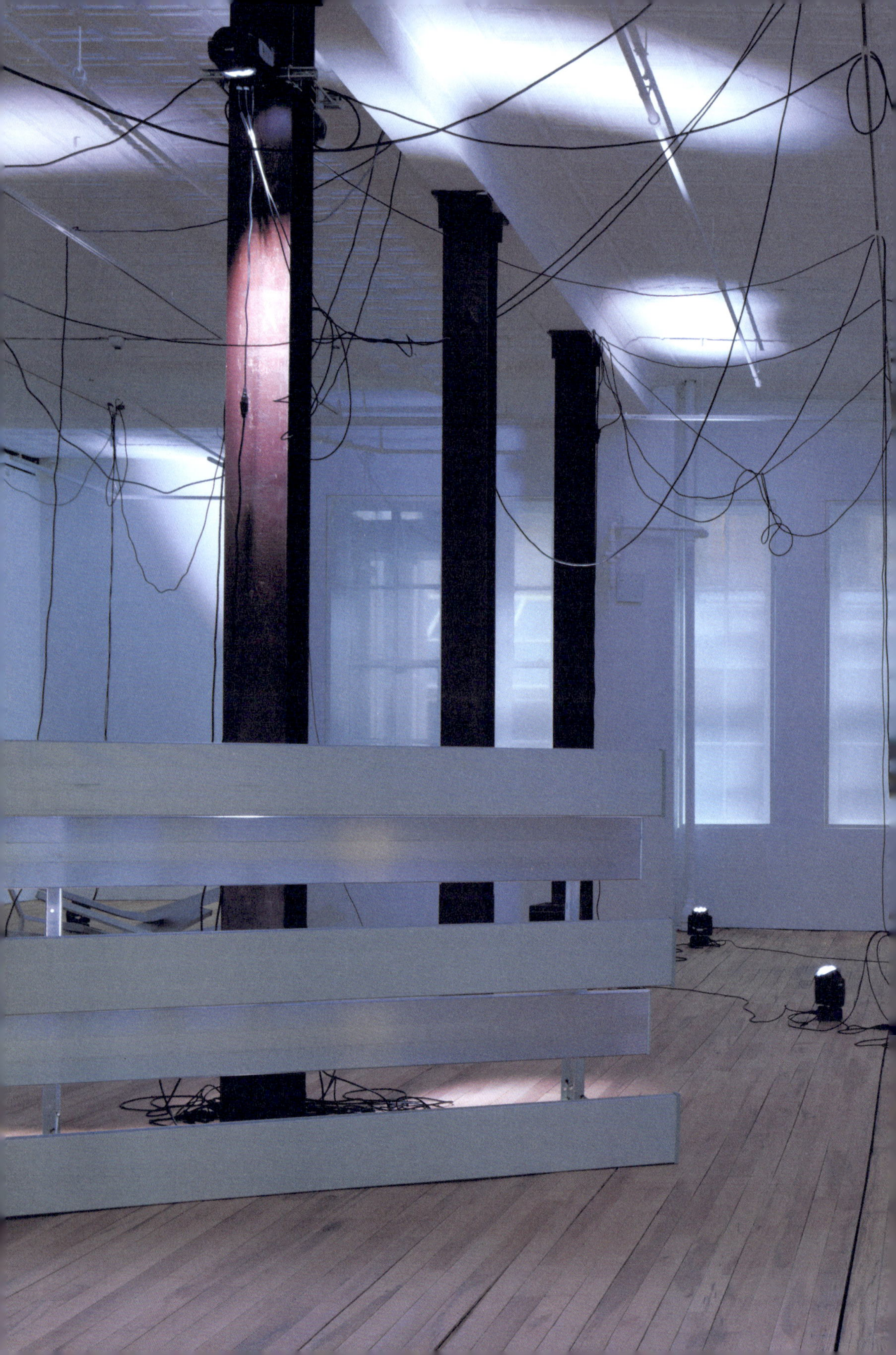

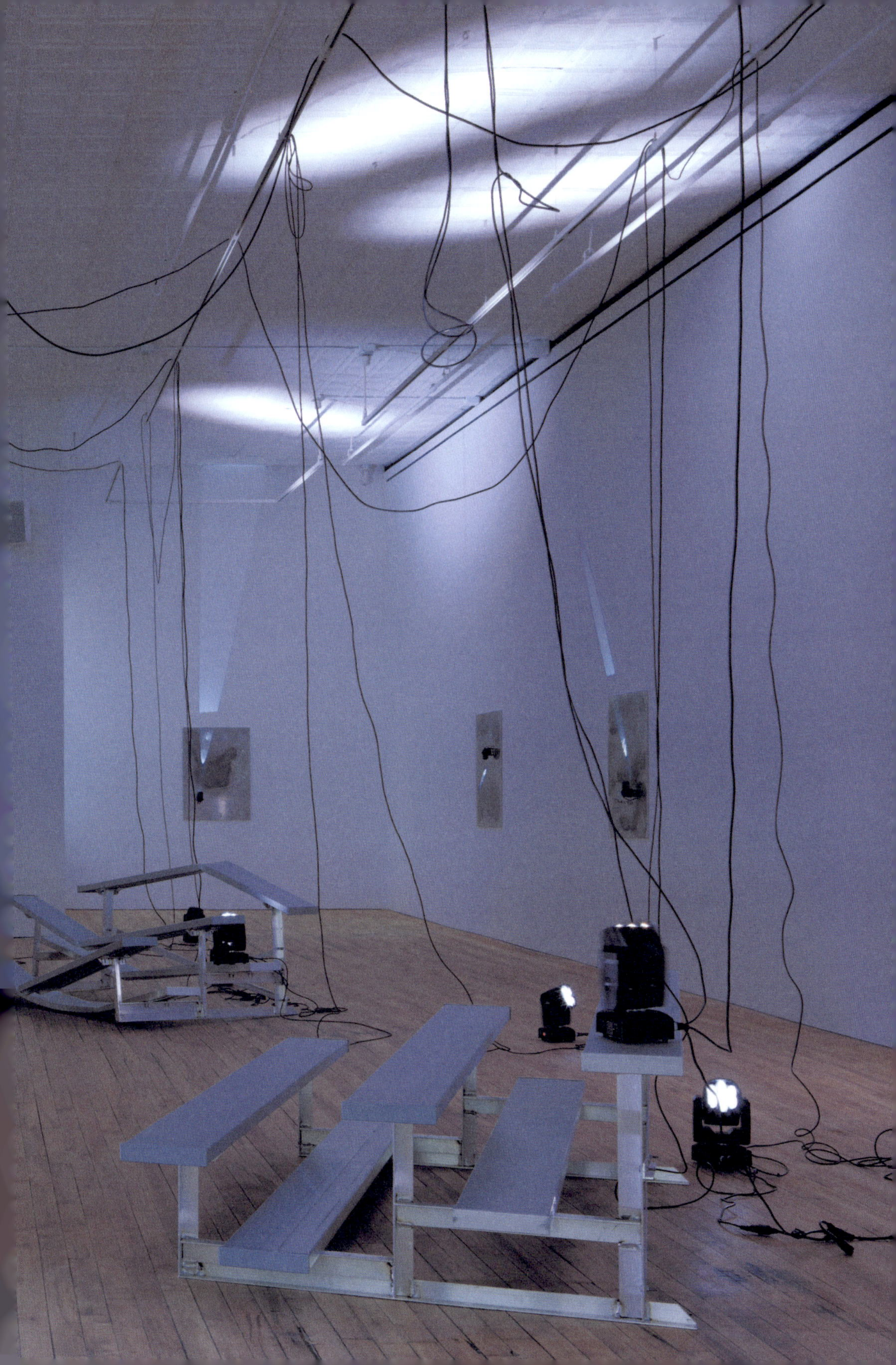

BODY PRINT: BRAIN, 2022
Stain, etching, and LED spotlight on aluminum panel
40 × 30 × 4 ½ inches | 101.6 × 76.2 × 11.4 cm

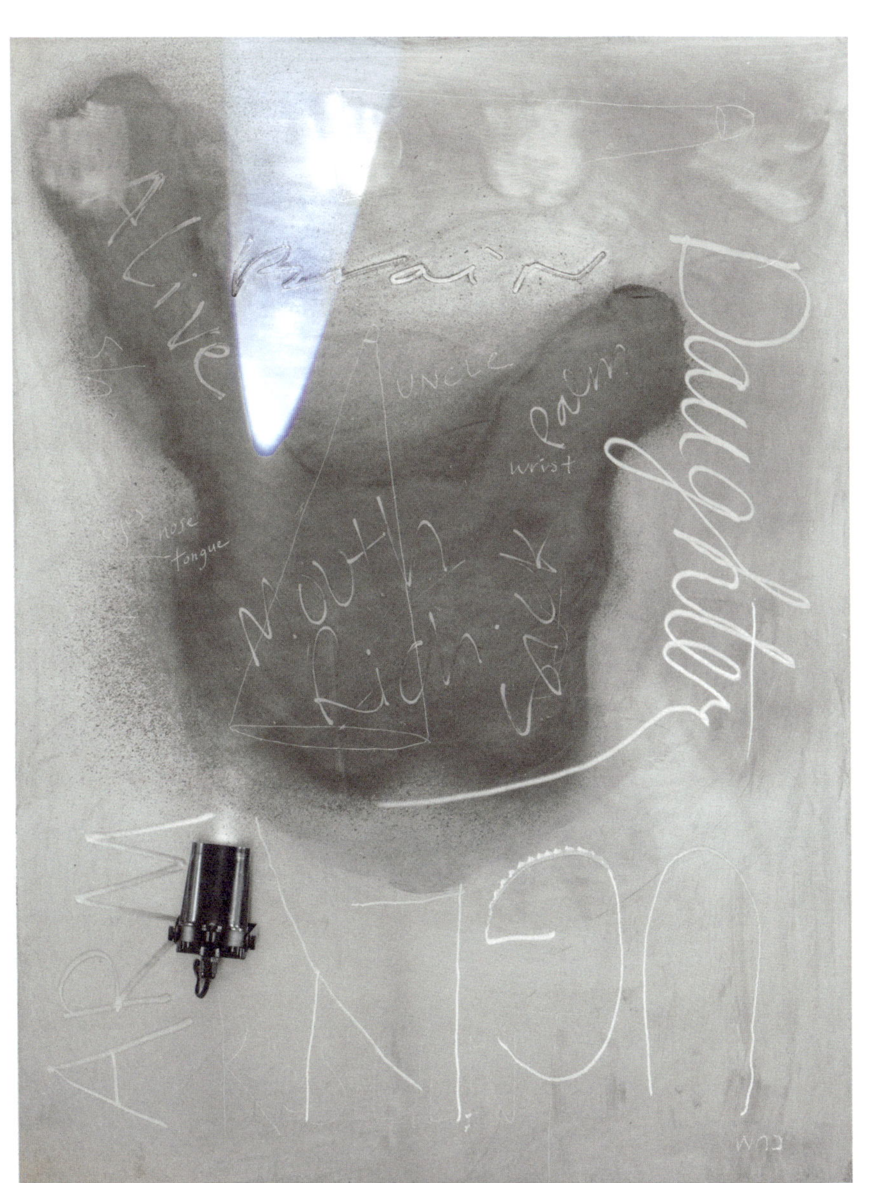
Alive
pain
Daughter
uncle
pain
wrist
eyes
nose
tongue
mouth
Right calf
ARM

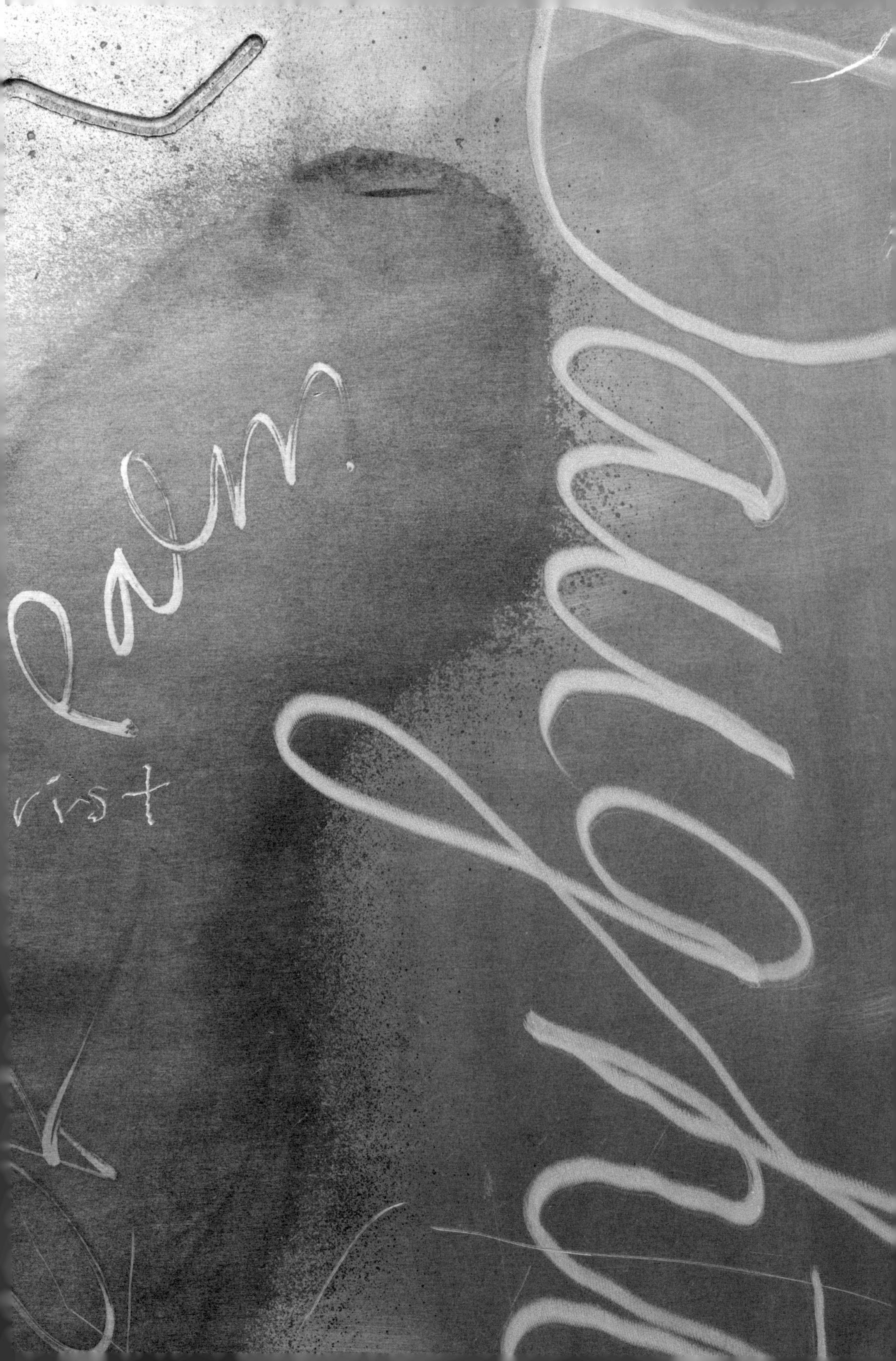

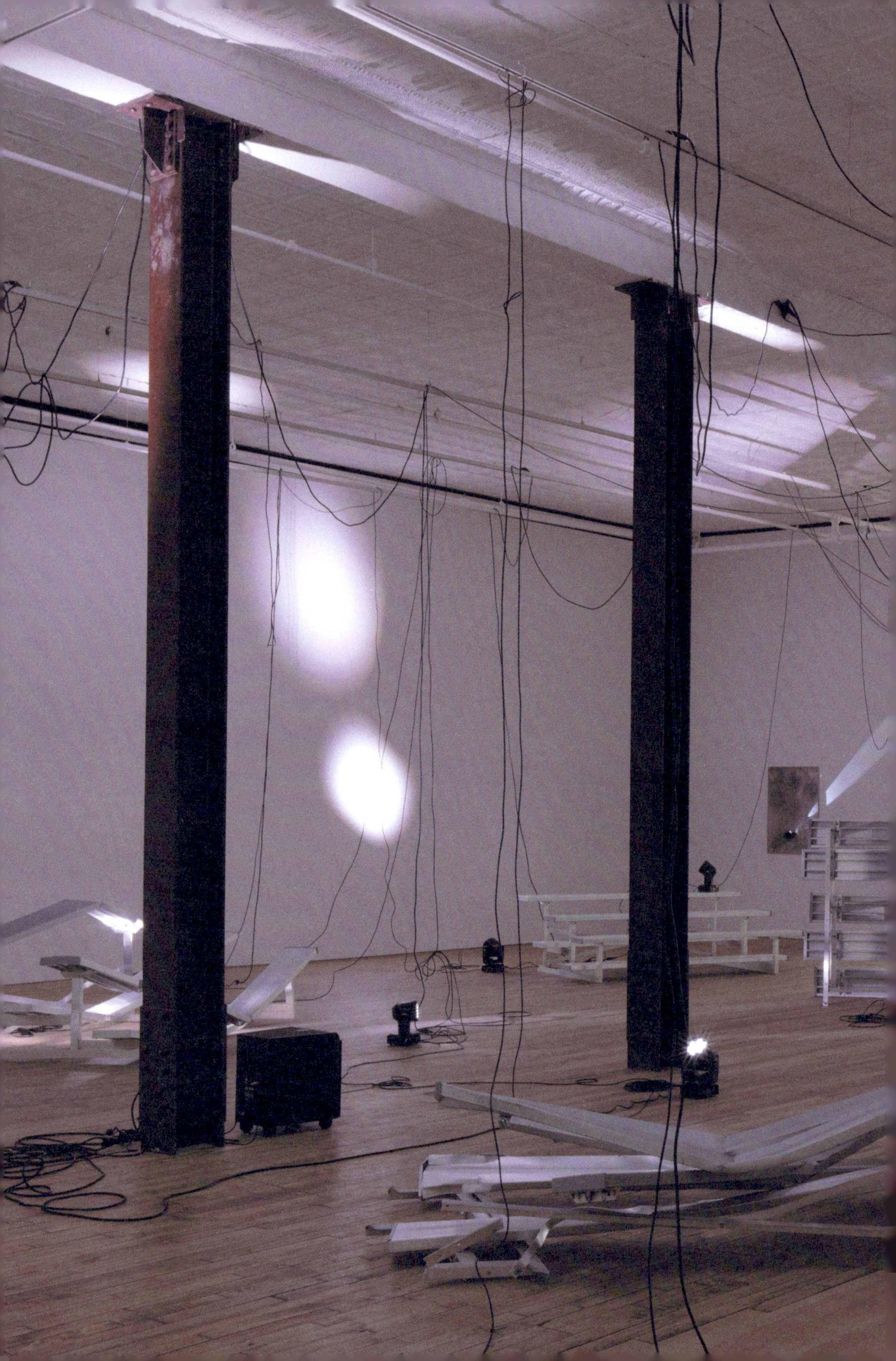

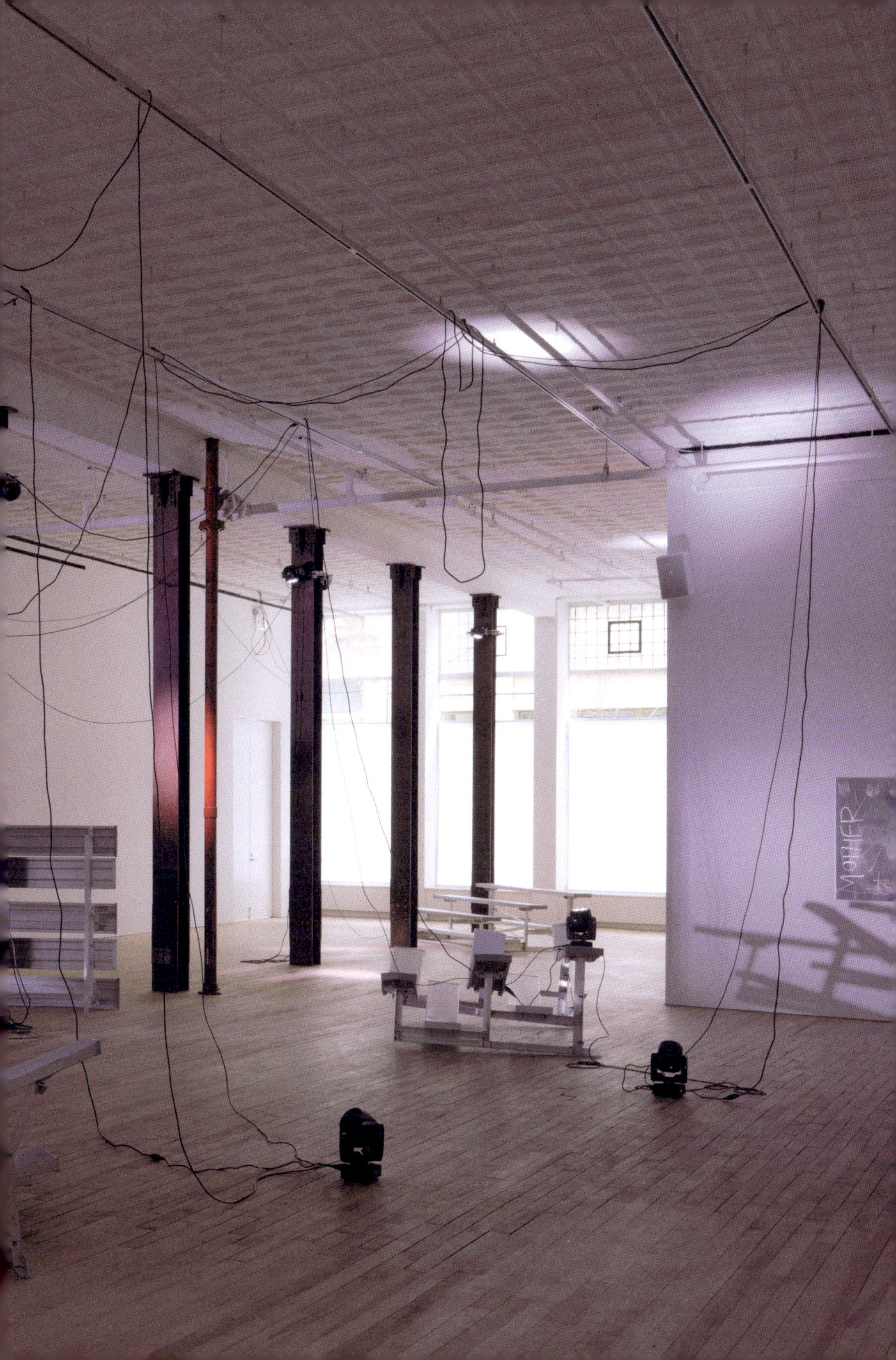

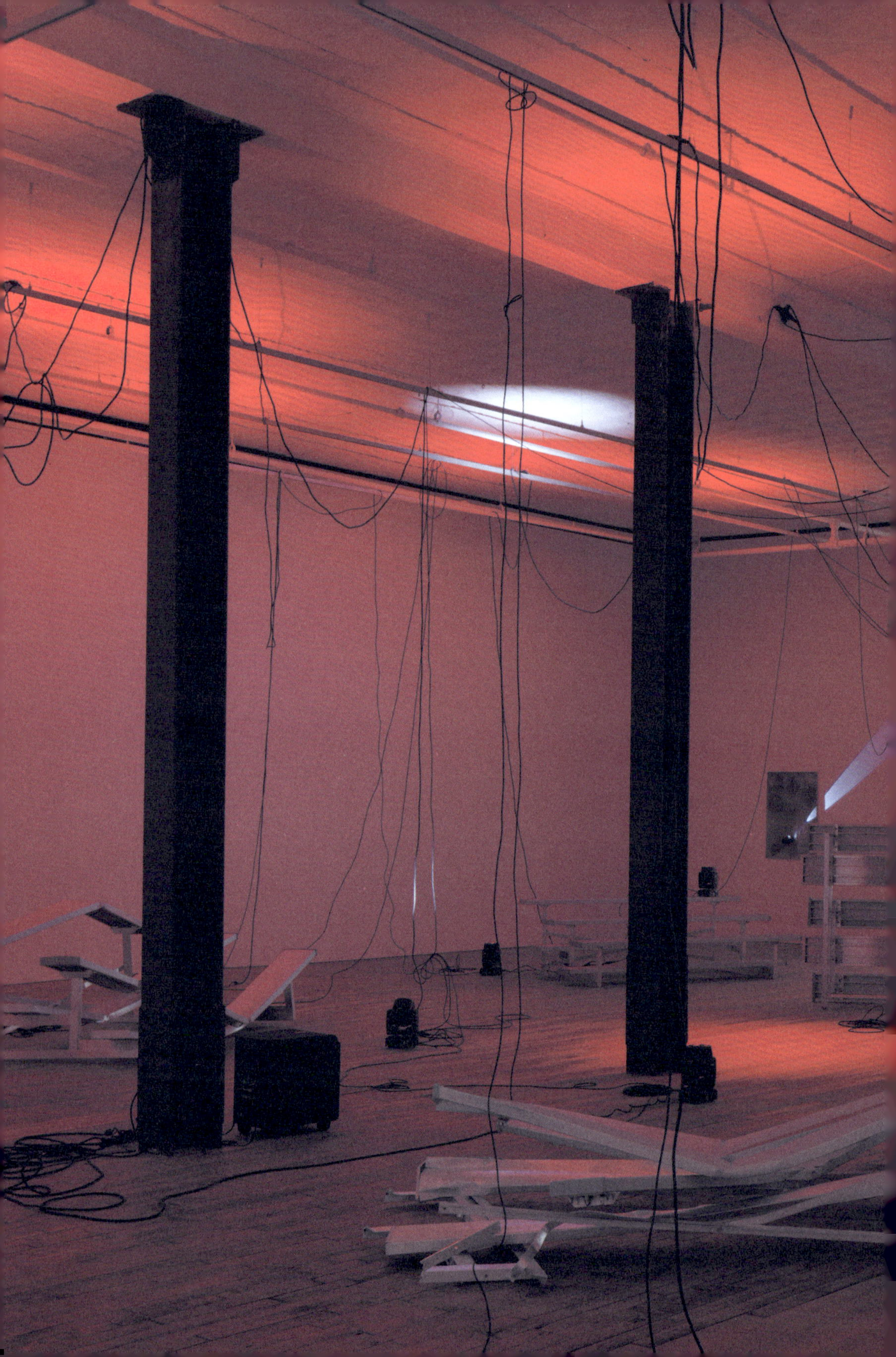

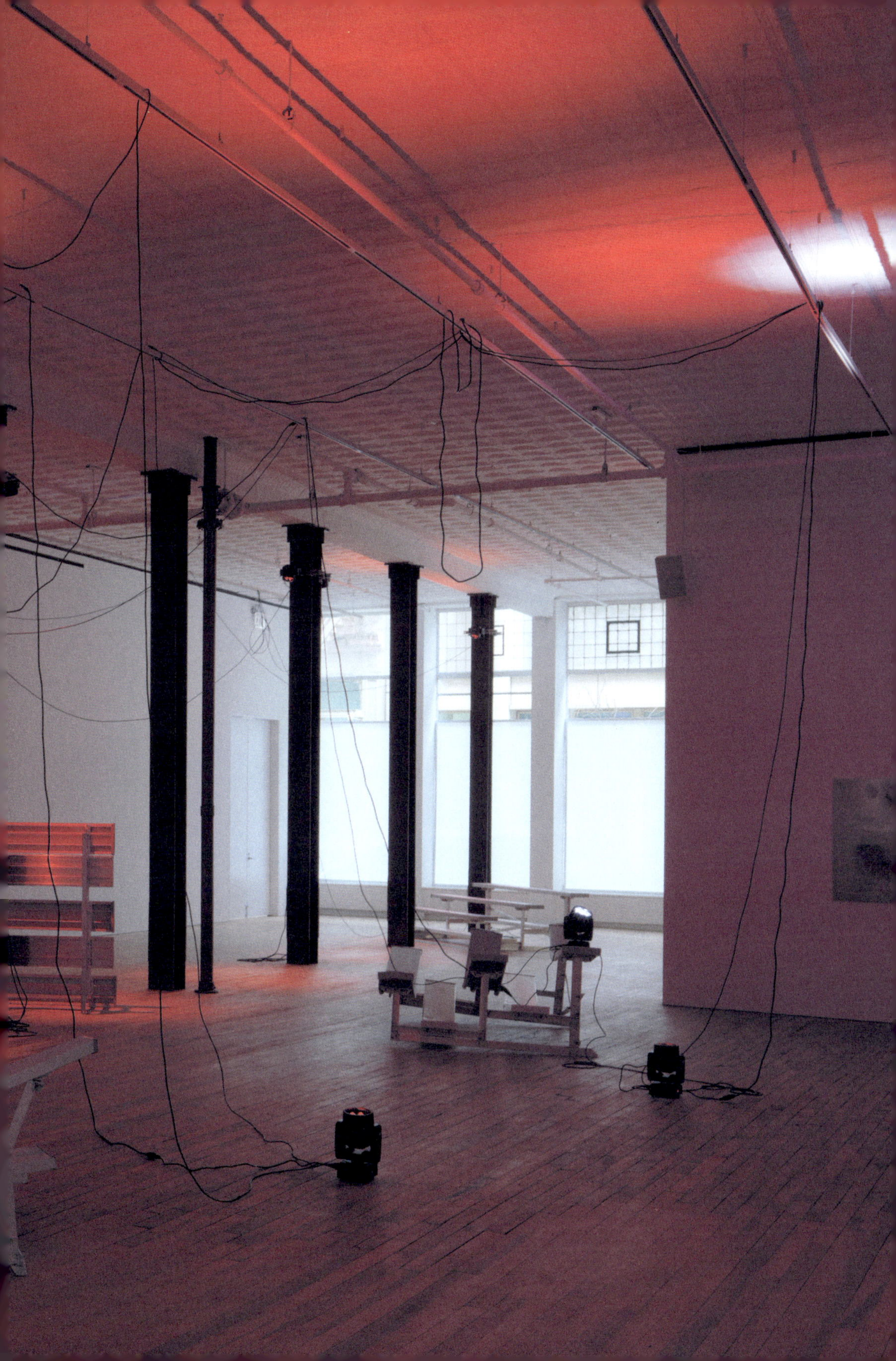

BODY PRINT: BLOOD, 2022
Stain, etching, and LED spotlight on aluminum panel
40 × 30 × 4 ½ inches | 101.6 × 76.2 × 11.4 cm

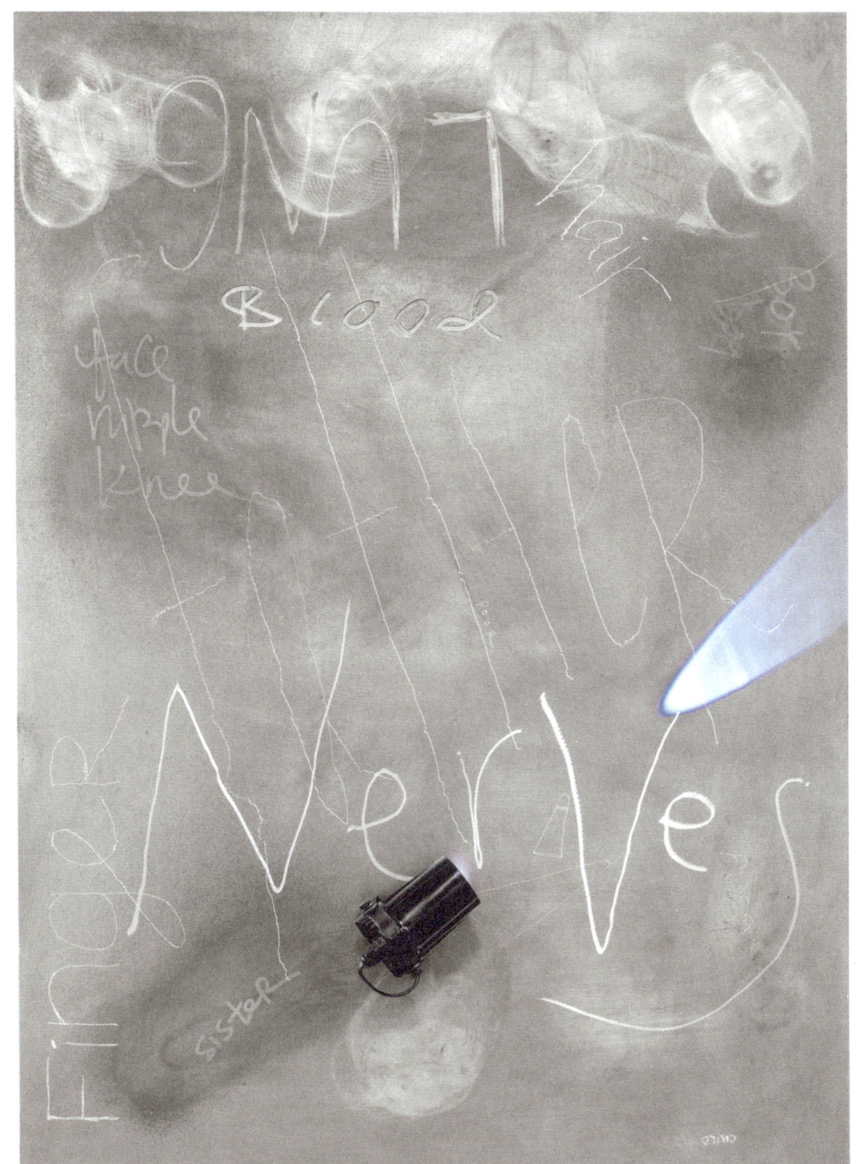
DON'T
hair
Blood
Boy
face
nipple
knee
FingeR
NerVes
sister
CHILD

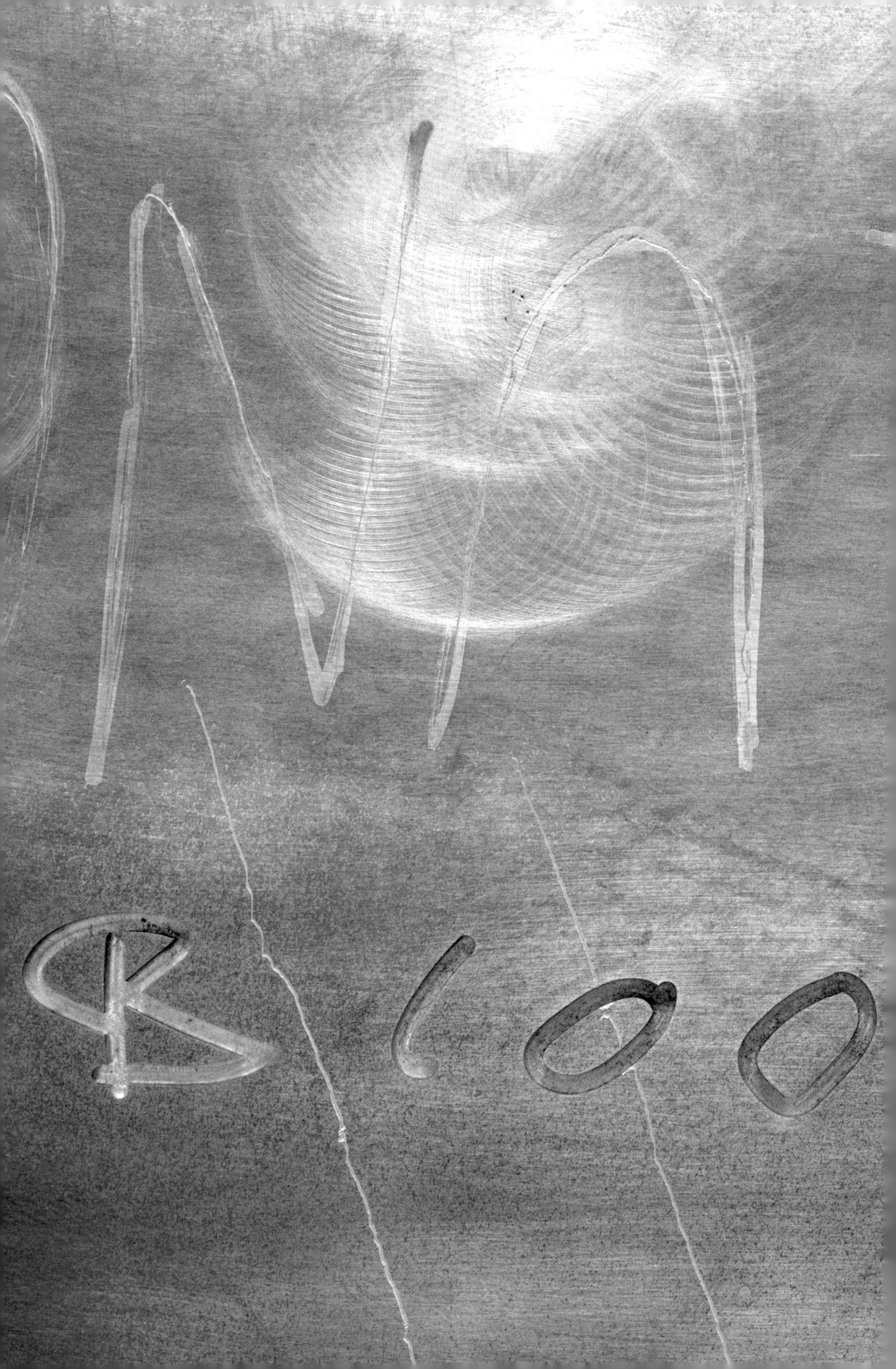

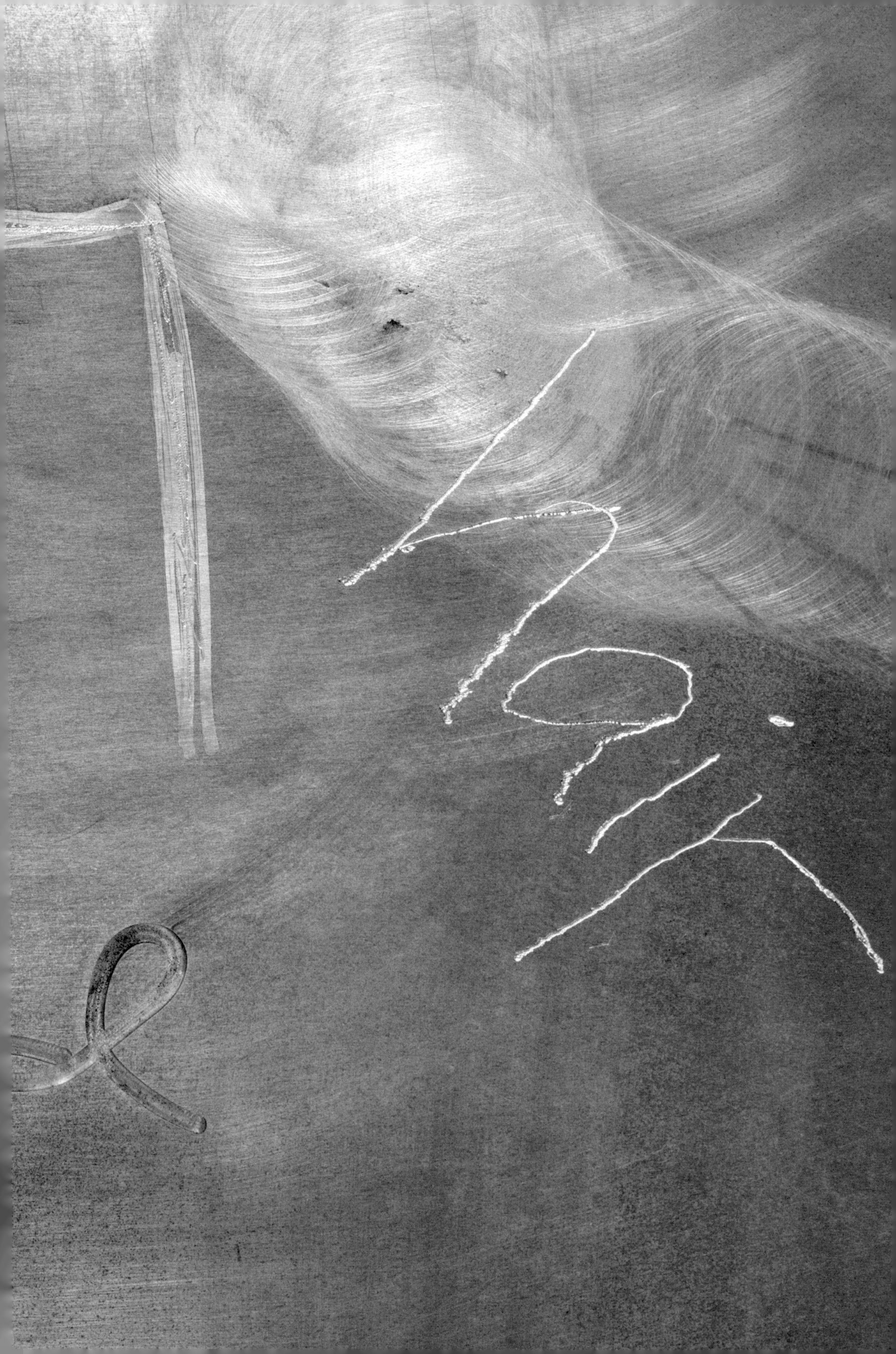

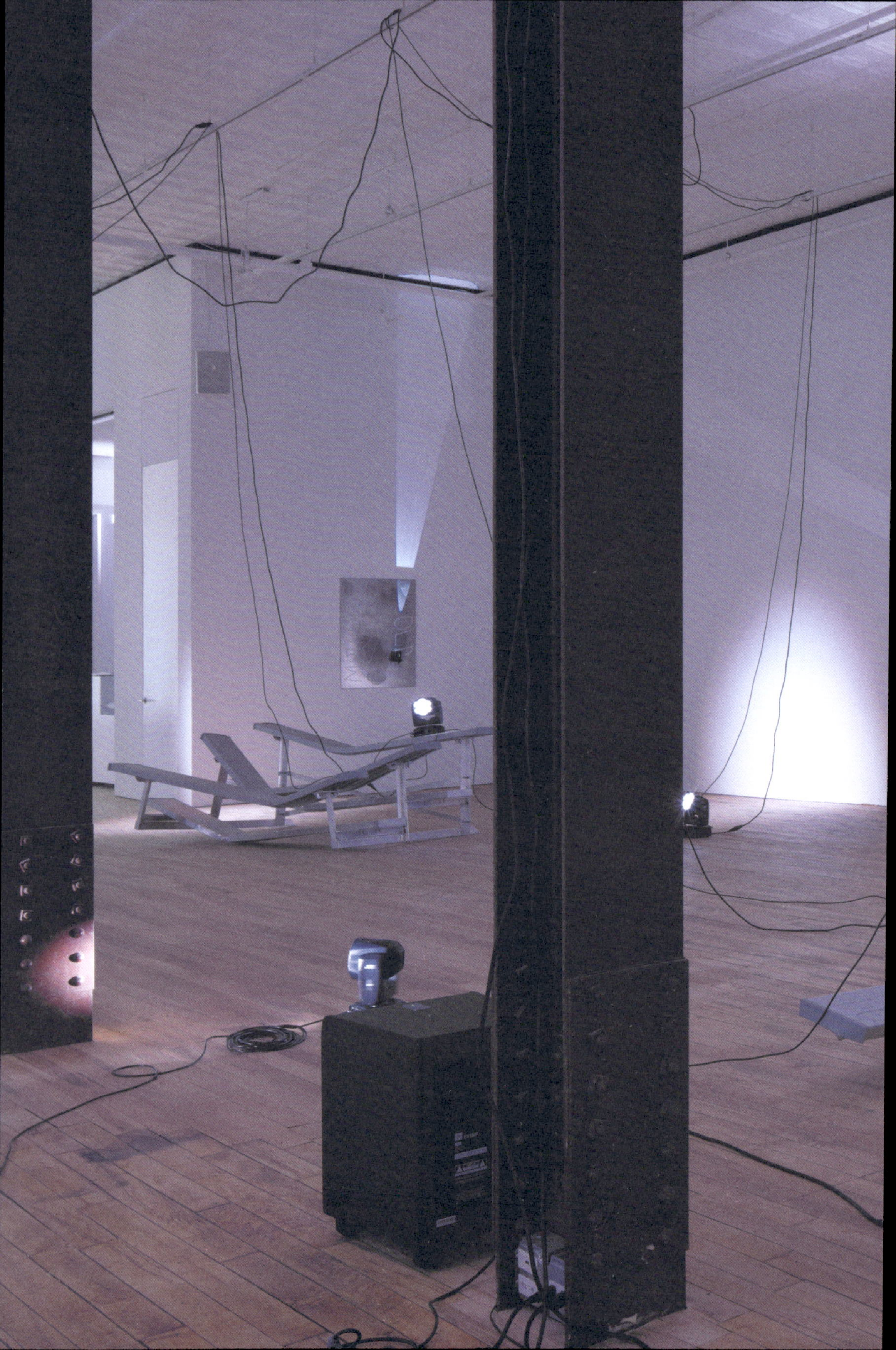

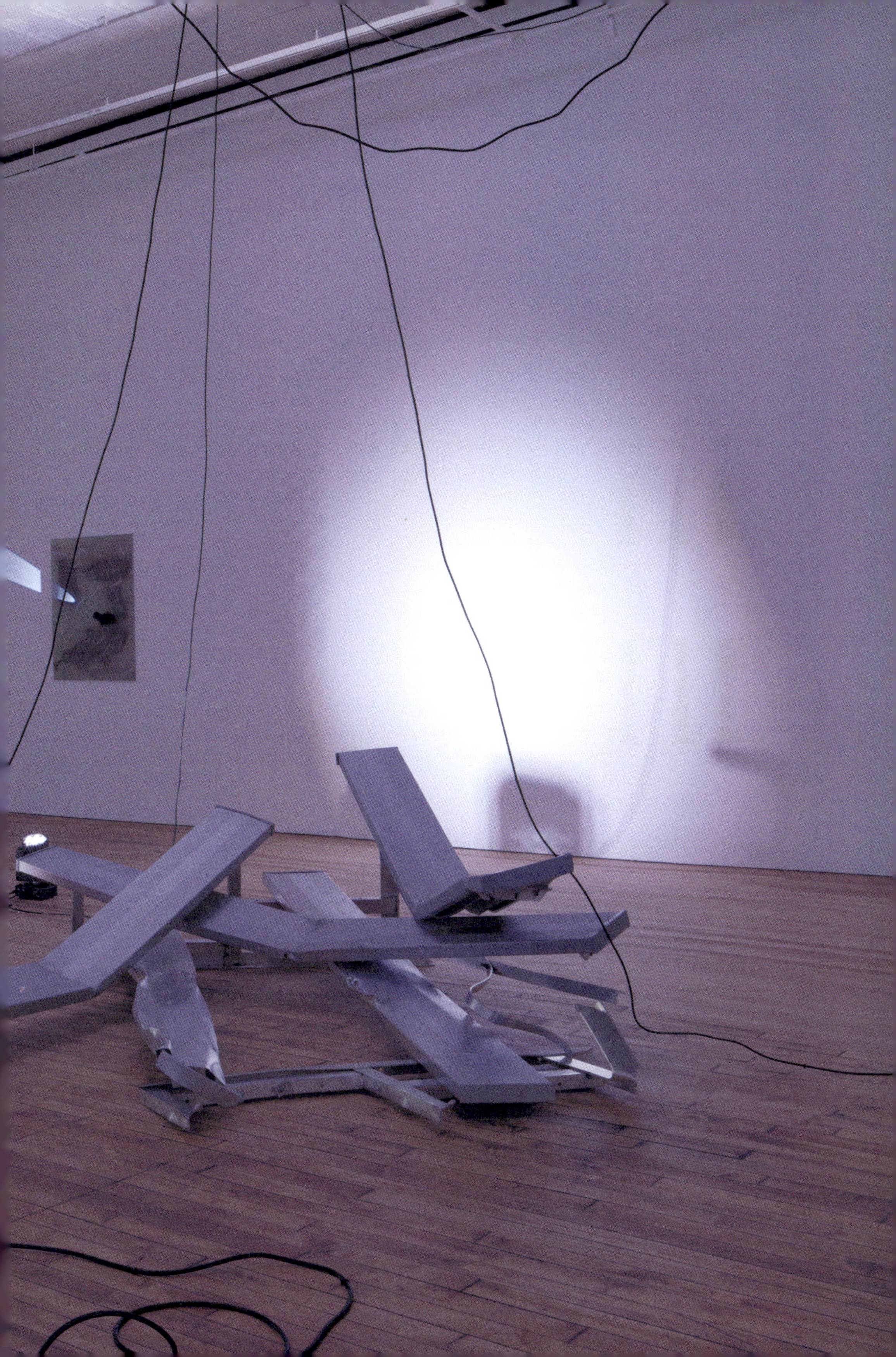

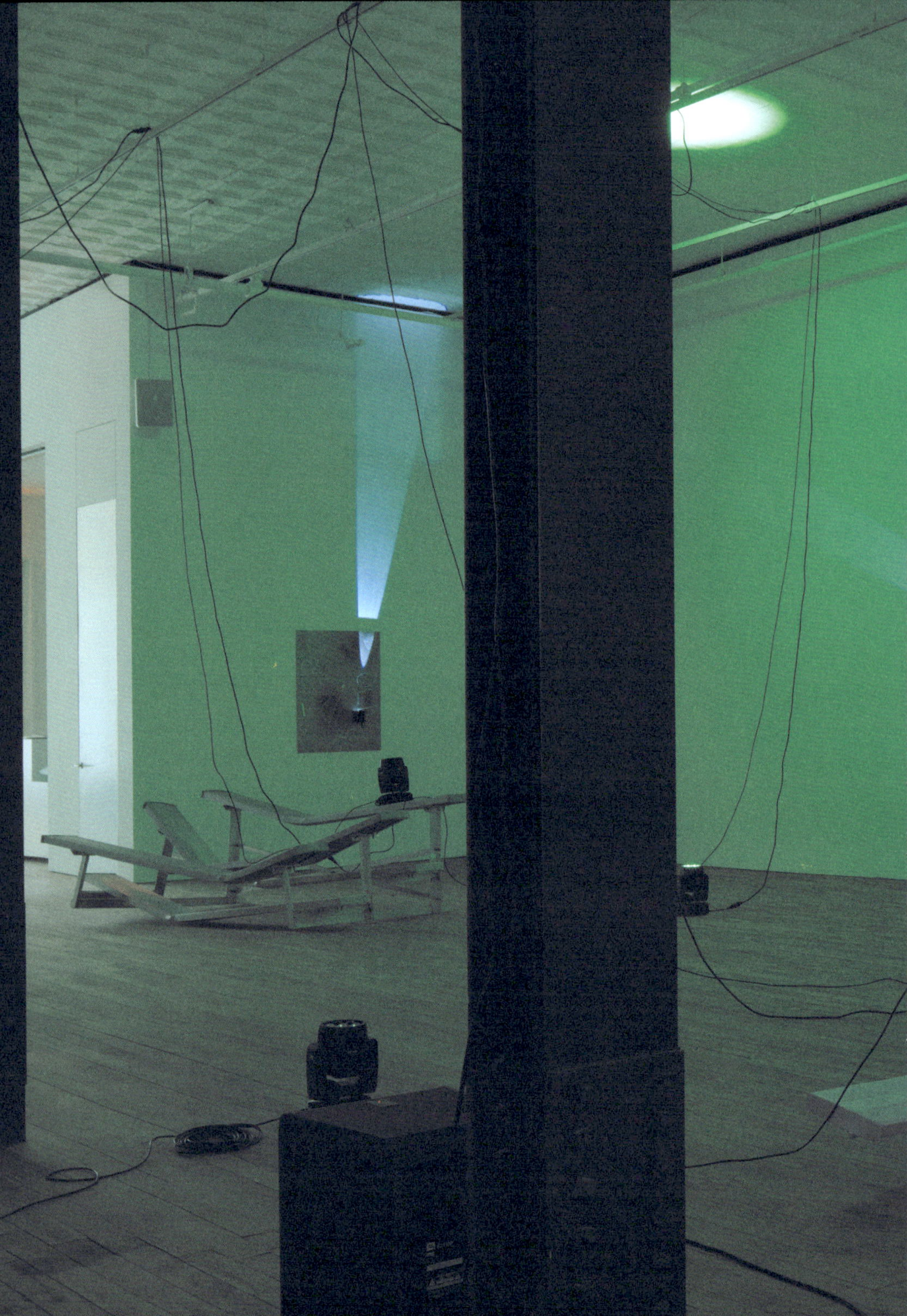

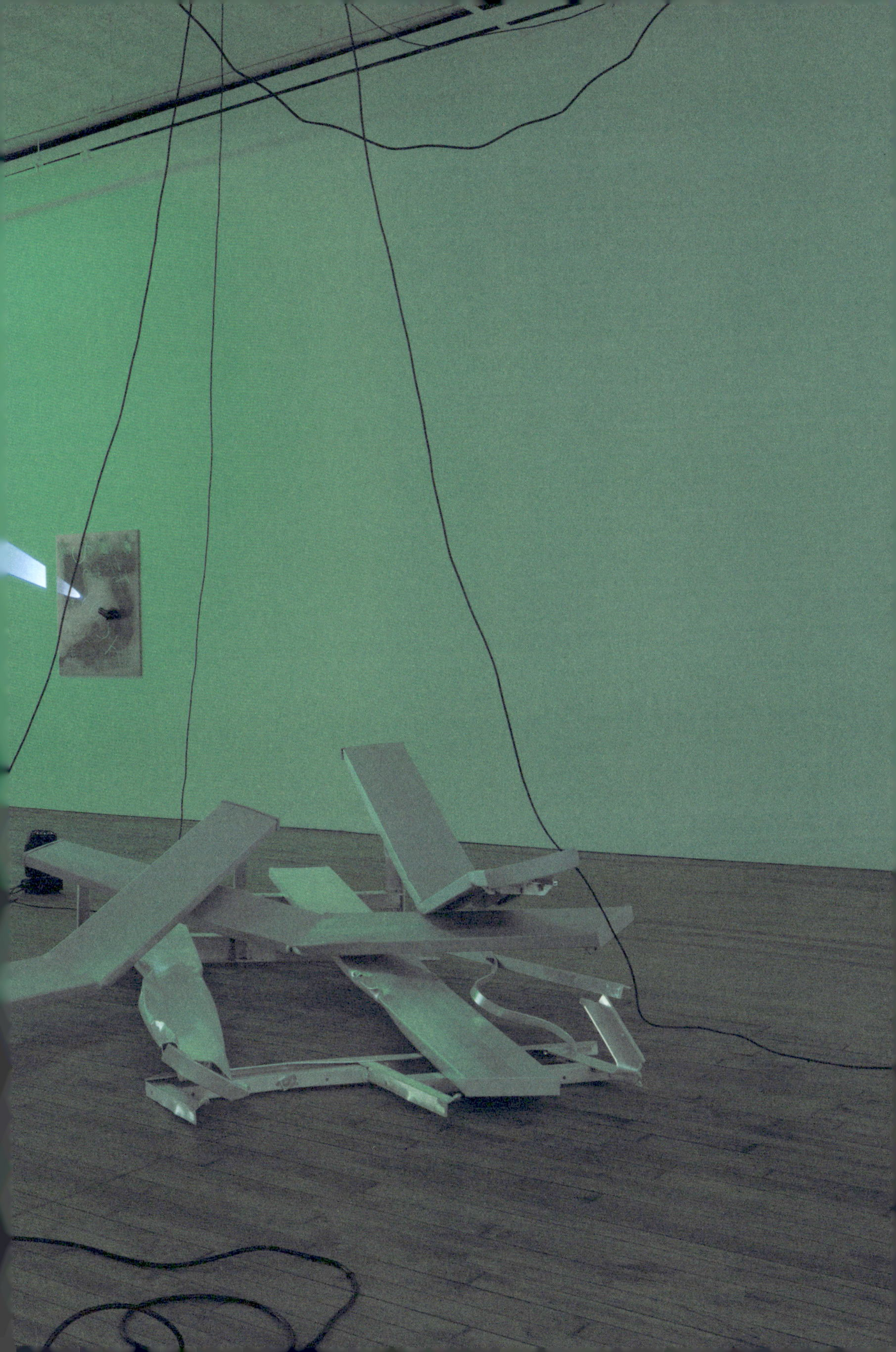

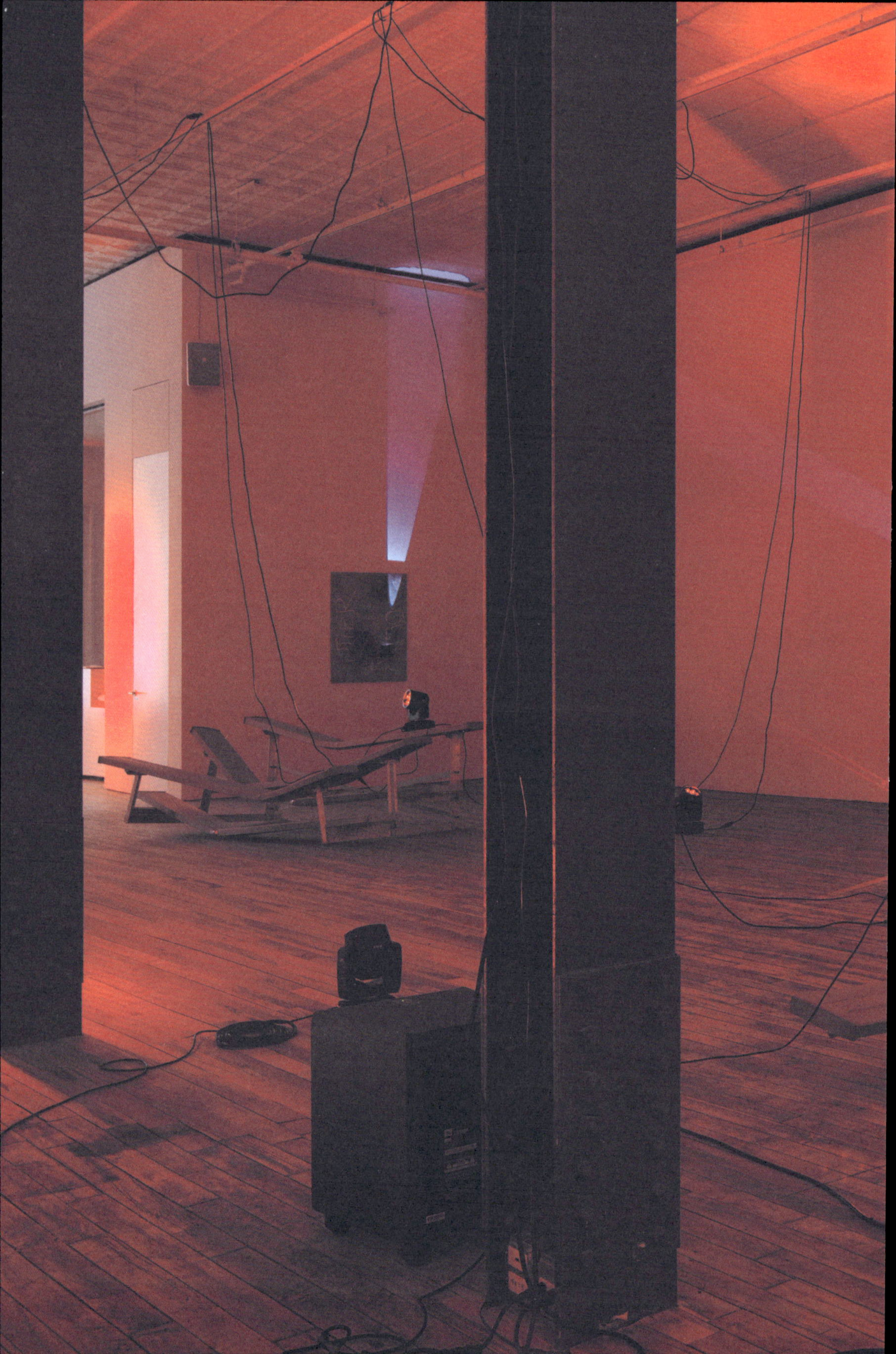

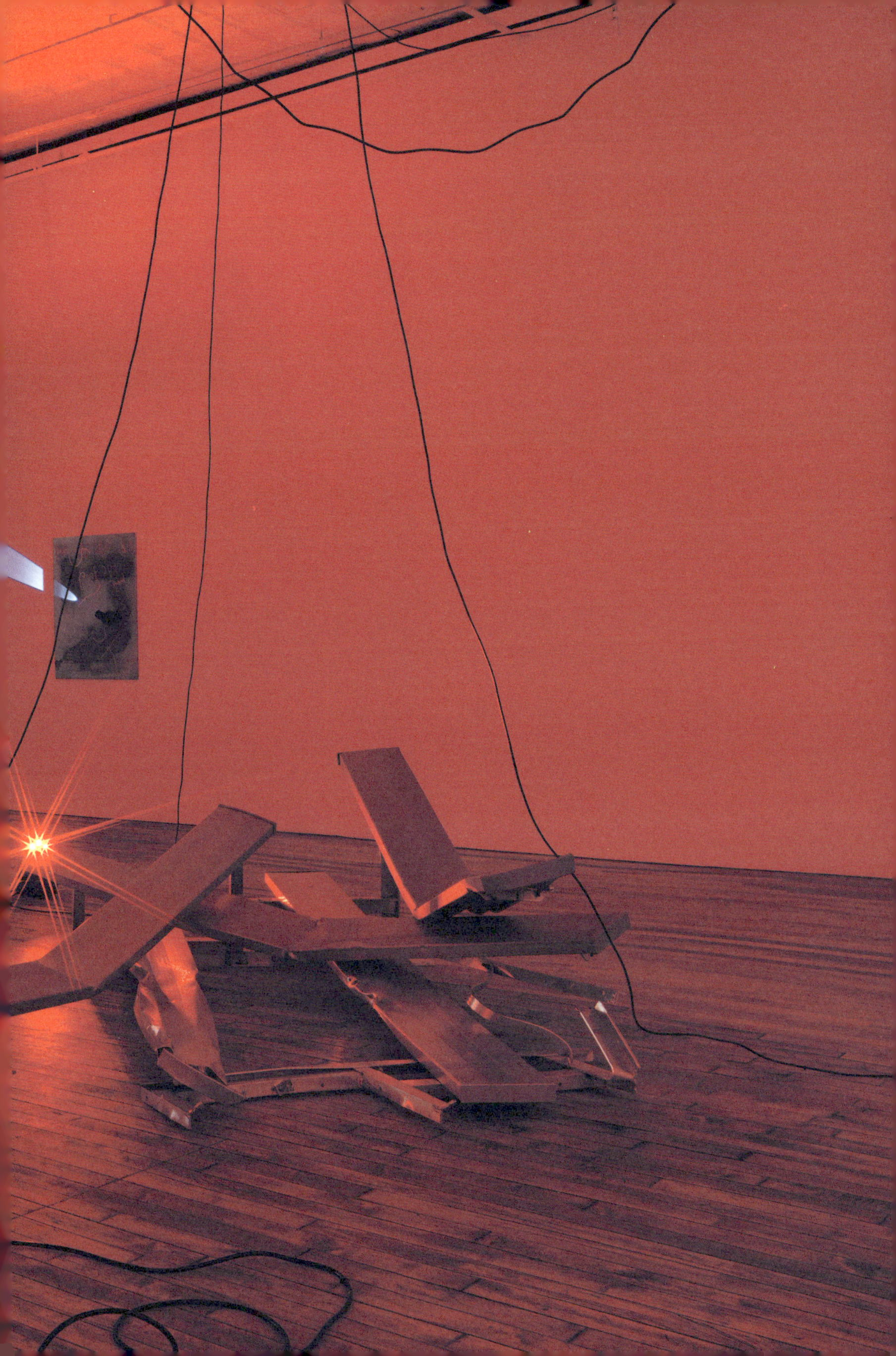

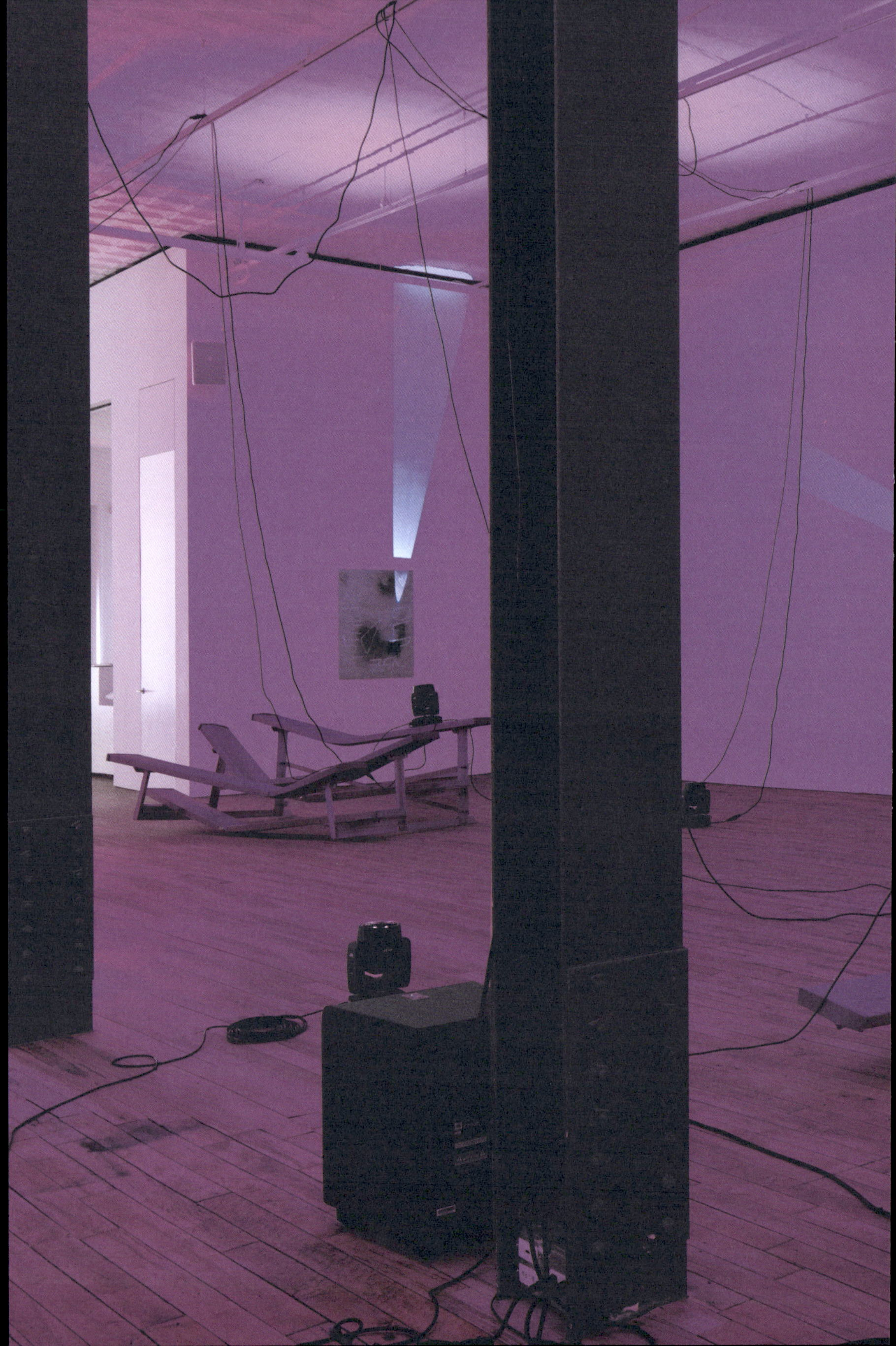

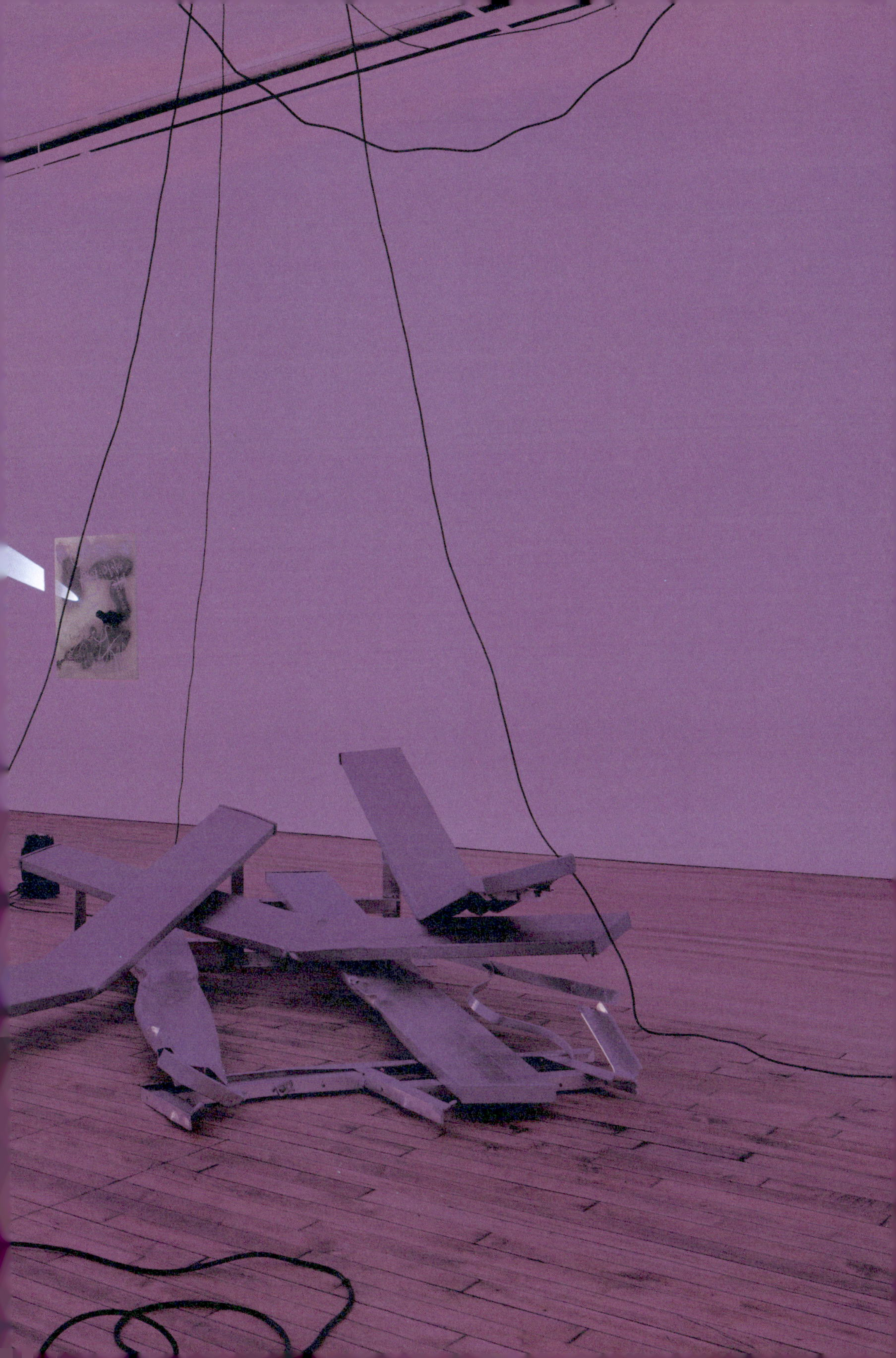

Suite for Tina Turner
Harmony Holiday

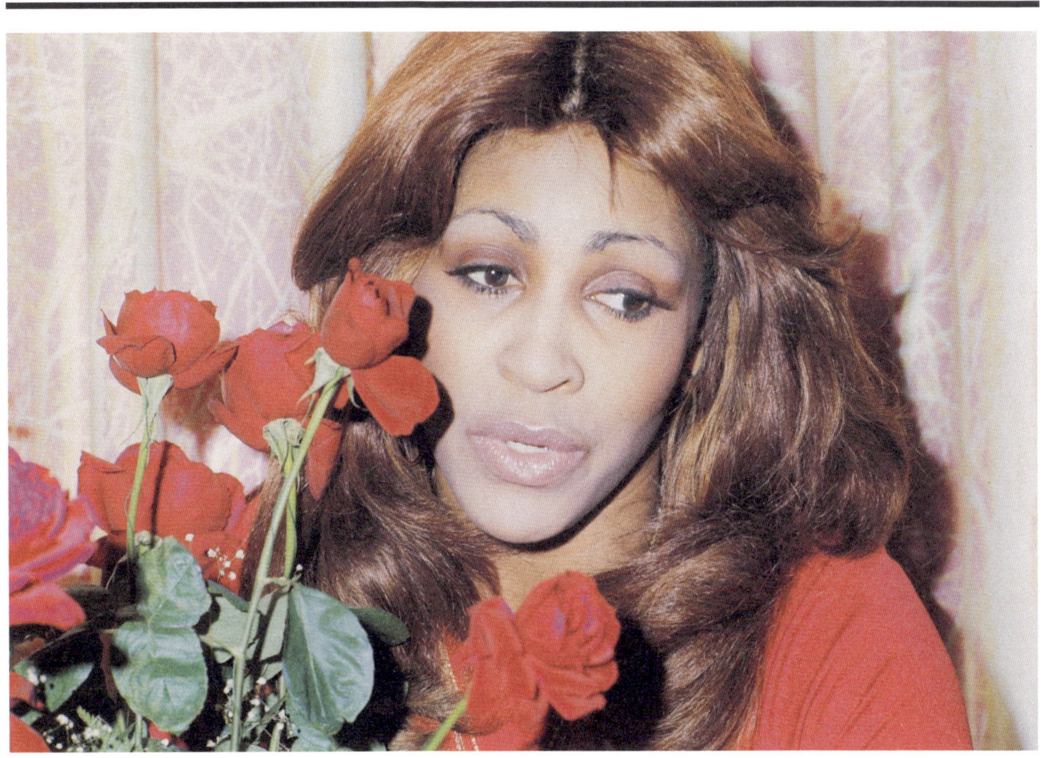

Granite City

Another   sundown wig on   the ground   dragging limp-leashed   headless bob

  neck
 in
 the
tree

with the veins   still   bulging   where she   would   be   hitting high   notes on *Down in the Valley*
Skull on   the   ground   neck   in   the   tree   it's   customary   Sister Mary   customer in her
own   life   but   this   isn't   her   only   life   just   an   alibi   for   the   razor
  Lacerating   craze   with   platform

Every   arousal has   a   little bit   of   threat   in   it   take   this   short road
Could   end   up   a   millionaire   could   be   the   slow   lane   beyond   the   body

Dishpan full of knives outside   the club   looking for justice

The courthouse has about it the simple   air   of failure

Got in trouble   there   where   we did   cotton   but   meant   unless I get a chance to kill him   first

One of the great dumb   transfigurations

Hold my name

Strawberries, Radio Formats

I think about becoming scarce   like the tickle of that fuzzy nudging of cotton on the palm

I could muster ghosts of hypervisibility   choke on my sleep   in a friendly way   bye, bye, baby

This last dream queen scream   might   be your   hit **(music here)** maybe

    and you can retire   fuck all the bitches you please

Traumatize   the children   as you wish   you   sick piece of shit anheroic misfit   with so

much blank   hatred in your eyes spilling   out   as   music   I did   love   you   I did collapse

and let my   pulse   fade into   your   desperate   threats   come back laughing   to myself as you begged

me to save you   from my death   If that isn't   love   it's   hate at least   close   enough

approximation
                        Do I go feral or farewell   clicking or   slitting

In   the best dream the pool   was covered in a thin layer of glass   and he jumped in

The water turned   the   dense petty red of his ugly blood and as the glass cracked there were

angels clapping   jostling me awake before dawn   so I could sing with them

I want a man without shame

Those were the days when a black man's damage   and how we nursed him back   to   unprovoked self-
sabotage was all that mattered.   Battered woman   battery lady   good wife   happy spade
And it was regular   to go   on stage bloody singing through   swollen lips   a little stolen mistress, veneers
so thick they reverberate instead of crack with the punches   he punched me in face and wild irises
bloomed, see   I can incorporate flowers   sing pretty and   soft   *we don't do anything nice and easy*
was a plea   in the speech but   I could make it   myth   for   him. I'm saying those were the days
when the dominant black myth   was that our men   were   so   wounded   we had to take   the erratic
violence   as it came   massage their   heads after each episode   to abate whatever incommunicable
pain caused them to try and kill us, the black women at home   waiting   with slaughterhouse gazes. I
worked on putting the smile   back into my eyes when I started chanting but it never   returned
completely. Maybe never was there in my mauve   colored maudlin   air.   I told myself   I was
protecting a genius   I was really guarding a monster   an accomplice   a stolen life   it's
nice to   know I had to be a   little sick and evil   to go along   makes it easy   to forgive
and nuzzle my memory of   those early   days of awe and pedestal   making   when my killer   was my
hero   at the country show   a blues balladeer   knocking   some   dreams out   of me   maybe we'll
run   hand in hand through   summer rain in the afterlife   sweet tears of forgiveness that shine
like smiles in   our eyes. He died   in   a studio fire   I went to Switzerland   to disappear

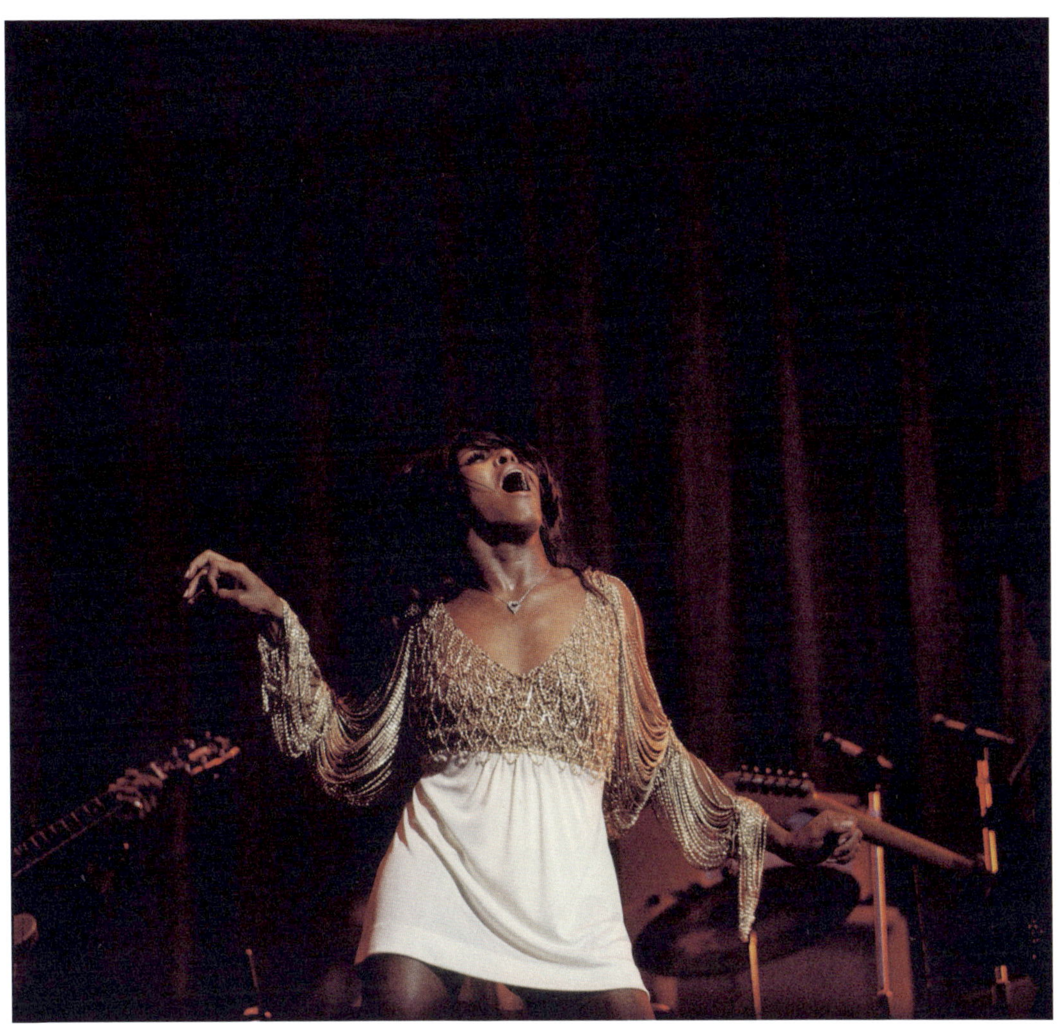

this is a mixed-up crucifixion   in glitz

Standing on top of all that music

The clown in the gleam   keeps grinning a dug up ambrosiaed blood of runaway so much   I'm nowhere
Organs failing to a skit of lights   as   we scream   our way to fainting   feigning   numb thing   all that pain
What a numb   and perfect thing   all mine

Don't be embarrassed that you're your own mother

Or of the wound with its swooping sensation its gusts of bruised blood as   you tuck the one you came from into the come-up graveyard in your   favorite heart   and measure the incision with salt—   matador   hoofing   the   dust pacing the tour bus with fabric and clay   why don't   they love   me   enough to   kill me

Here I am working against time

If time is a form of compassion   we all agree upon love is sociopathic   never ending or beginning only happening   in   fists and screams   here   I   am   the time   he   redacted   and I split open   in   the song   a   black petaled   rose girl   friday   resurrection melody about   the   way—   How   we   dreaded the happiness   after a fix   its swift uncompromising jolt   of potential   the clarity after ruin   my jaundice   my stage   presence during and after   death   my   well-told yellow ledge   of perfumed cash as I collapsed   dogs and gods sniffing me like an empty   basket of horror candy   and how I would be scalped   and skipped into my   little emergency   like   star

Blues for Some Bones

Abrasive silence   sway the razor in some dimes into   faces   face up in some dimes   thumbed for
patience or comfort   our bodies confess   through wins   simps, liars   if this is how I look to look *like a*
million bucks   currency in   trouble   or whatever it takes to make some   blue near   the eye
  Another fist or a fuck suckling pollen   Ephesians something   or other   bucking   in   the   beam
swerving like snakes to   say   it

Braid me up   lay the wig so it stays   when I give into the moist palms   of maniac spectators   maybe
they're not   maniacs   maybe they're not watching my eyes bleed and clapping   at me

That all mine   not even minor mirror of pain   is what   I   trust   it knocks   shoves up on spines
shakes them   down to finally,
                              spindles
                                    and tells us we're   home

The quiet ones   held in by dignity   are the dead ones   now   held in by   stone clean cold   so cold
it feels wet   stings to pat and pedal   delve   and in the next world   they finally notice themselves
sobbing in   some sun blind corner   or giggling   and   skipping   with playmates   for money

No shame is better
You dream faster
Shadow addict   at   the door again strapped   and stripped
My night shift

Performance as Fugitive Space

How I catastrophized beauty   thought if it got too good it   would   become   a ruins   a creepy gravel of
devaluation of values   to   make   it   beyond   my   fear   of   the   good   life   of the fickle innuendo of
strife   hunting   here   I   go

We fear   our   own gratification   because

Pleasure feels like punishment because

I was so alienated   because

I felt so good   sober   felt   so   good on my knees in powder

Felt so good   in   snow and better   in   quartz   sand

Felt so loaded with   husbands and   other banners of nerve

interpreted as an instruction to break into singing
 It may mean forever

But what now sweetens the tongue must turn to terror

Coroner in the   dereliction   turning tricks tricks   not truce tricks   real ones   for a   taste of it

The general tone of this apocalypse is clear and sweet

Tina's Scream / Let me touch your mind

What I mostly remember is flashing lights   unabashed crescendo and my pulse   edging   in the center of his
scream I didn't   know   was   my   own   My dharma   my   best dilemma   some contrived belligerence I
didn't   know   was   accurate   mortar   in my throat grinding the vowels   into   get out   gags

It surprises even me how effortlessly I   clawed my   way through the language   of low love   in
tantrum   but made it   feel sweet   switching personas here   Ike and Tina had a bed
exactly   like my parents' bed   don't make   me grapple   or shatter in that   reckoning
Just take   it   as   a   detail   a   meticulous   thing about   cycles   velvet circles   we sleep in
for   style   and to signify one   large cosmic   bitch   I will   kill you   in your   slumber if
you   even   try   to leave me   eye   no one told you to mourn facts   that was your own

Pathetic inclination   a sign of an abundance   of self-regard   a habit   for close   looking   high
seeing   all seeing   obliterative eye   type   kiss   the   skylark type— our   way of resting in
a   pattern   of   moans   Is it traditional   for scared & violent men   to sleep in bull's
eye   is it why   I   came out   charging

David Zwirner and Ebony L. Haynes wish to thank Nikita Gale, without whom this exhibition and publication would not have been possible. Thanks are due to Andrea Fraser for her thought-provoking program and essay and to Harmony Holiday for her moving suite of poems. We would also like to thank Daphne Brooks.

For their work on the exhibition, we are grateful to Rebecca Ashby-Colón, Claire Ball, Susan Cernek, Allison Chipak, Ojive DeLungéla, Felice Jiang, Coco Kim, Vida Lercari, Thomas Ling, Julia Lukacher, Alyssa Mattocks, Kerry McFate, Sean Morgan, Clive Murphy, Julian Phillips, Kyle Rafferty, Robert Richburg, Gabriela Scopazzi, Janna Singer-Baefsky, Virginia Stroh, and Nora Woodin.

Thank you to Andrea Hyde for the catalogue series design and, for their work on this volume, to Claire Bidwell, Sergio Brunelli, Luke Chase, Fabio Ferrandini, Zeno Ferrandini, Doro Globus, Elizabeth Gordon, Amy Hordes, Jessica Palinski, Mari Perina, Chris Peterson, Magnus Schaefer, Molly Stein, Jules Thomson, Joey Young, and Lucas Zwirner.

The artist would like to thank 56 Henry, Mack Allan, Lily Brooks-Dalton, Hana Cohn, Commonwealth and Council, Rufus and veronique d'entremont, Mainstay Fabrication, Reyes | Finn, Elon Schoenholz, Dane Scott, Graham Stewart, Marisa Tatum-Taylor, Ana "Veva" Véjar, Tashi Wada, Josephine Wang, and Corie Yaguchi.

Collections

p. 29: Zabludowicz Collection
p. 33: Collection of Paul Leong
p. 41: Private collection, New York
p. 49: Museum of Fine Arts, Boston. Stephen D. and
Susan W. Paine Acquisition Fund for 20th Century
and Contemporary Art
p. 57: The Mohn Family Trust Collection
p. 65: Private collection, Maryland

Photography

pp. 22–23, 24–25, 26–27, 29, 30–31, 33, 34–35, 36–37, 38–39,
44–45, 46–47, 49, 50–51, 52–53, 54–55, 57, 59, 60–61, 62–63,
65, 66–67, 68–69, 70–71, 72–73, 74–75: Kerry McFate
pp. 41, 43: Elon Schoenholz
p. 77: Lynn Goldsmith/Corbis Historical/VCG via Getty Images
p. 81: David Redfern/Redferns via Getty Images

The *Clarion* series is an essential component of 52 Walker programming. An edition will accompany every exhibition, highlighting and expanding on the show's conceptual theses through newly commissioned texts, interviews, archival materials, and artistic interventions. The series is named in honor of the renowned author Octavia E. Butler, who was first published in the 1971 Clarion Science Fiction and Fantasy Writers' Workshop anthology.

Other Titles in the *Clarion* Series
I. Kandis Williams: A Line

Forthcoming Titles
III. Nora Turato: govern me harder
IV. Tiona Nekkia McClodden: MASK / CONCEAL / CARRY

Published by David Zwirner Books
on the occasion of

Nikita Gale: END OF SUBJECT
52 Walker, 52 Walker Street, New York
January 21–March 26, 2022

David Zwirner Books
529 West 20th Street, 2nd Floor
New York, New York 10011
+1 212 727 2070
davidzwirnerbooks.com

Editor: Ebony L. Haynes
Project Editor: Jessica Palinski
Proofreaders: Chris Peterson, Magnus Schaefer

Design: Andrea Hyde
Photography Coordinators: Rebecca Ashby-Colón, Allison Chipak, Virginia Stroh
Production: Luke Chase, Jules Thomson
Color separations: VeronaLibri, Verona
Printing: VeronaLibri, Verona

Typefaces: DTL Fleischmann, Genath, F Grotesk
Paper: Magno Natural, 140 gsm

Publication © 2023 David Zwirner Books

ISBN 978-1-64423-074-9

Library of Congress Control Number: 2022911361

Printed in Italy

Notes

Notes

Notes